I0477329

A COLLECTION OF SERVICE ESSAYS

A Practical Approach

HARRY KATZAN JR
A COLLECTION OF SERVICE ESSAYS

A Practical Approach

A COLLECTION OF SERVICE ESSAYS

Copyright © 2018 Harry Katzan Jr.

All rights reserved. No part of this book may be used or reproduced by any means, graphic, electronic, or mechanical, including photocopying, recording, taping or by any information storage retrieval system without the written permission of the author except in the case of brief quotations embodied in critical articles and reviews.

iUniverse books may be ordered through booksellers or by contacting:

iUniverse
1663 Liberty Drive
Bloomington, IN 47403
www.iuniverse.com
1-800-Authors (1-800-288-4677)

Because of the dynamic nature of the Internet, any web addresses or links contained in this book may have changed since publication and may no longer be valid. The views expressed in this work are solely those of the author and do not necessarily reflect the views of the publisher, and the publisher hereby disclaims any responsibility for them.

Any people depicted in stock imagery provided by Getty Images are models, and such images are being used for illustrative purposes only. Certain stock imagery © Getty Images.

ISBN: 978-1-5320-4276-8 (sc)
ISBN: 978-1-5320-4278-2 (hc)
ISBN: 978-1-5320-4277-5 (e)

Library of Congress Control Number: 2018902218

Print information available on the last page.

iUniverse rev. date: 02/22/2018

Contents

A service is a client/provider interaction that creates and captures value for both participants. It is a multidisciplinary subject that studies the interaction of strategy, process, people/workforce, and underlying technology. The concepts of service are related to information technology since that discipline is an enabler for aligning technology with persons and organizations. This report covers the key elements of service and explores its relationship with related academic subjects.

In the execution of a service event, quality is everything. When clients and providers interact to create and capture value, they are engaging in a process known as *social constructionism*, which focuses on the ways in which individuals and groups participate in the creation of their perceived reality. This essay argues that clients can, or perhaps should, control the efficacy of value creation through service quality assessment. The concepts of social constructionism, service systems, value determination, and quality assessment are covered. The application of social constructionism to service systems has not been covered before.

This essay gives a conspectus of Service and of Service Science for academicians and practitioners with the express purpose of defining the scope of the discipline. The subject of services is the up and coming discipline for the 21st century, and it encompasses technology, entrepreneurship, business growth, and innovation – four subjects that are generally of interest to most managers and scientists, alike. Services are important to people in business, government, education, health care and management, religion, military, scientific research, engineering, and other endeavors that are too numerous to mention, because most service providers – be they individuals, businesses, governments, and so forth – are also consumers of services. This is the first of three introductory papers on the subject. The second essay, entitled "Service Management and Business," covers the operational environment for services, and the final essay, entitled "Service Technology and Architecture," covers the technical and architectural basis for the Service discipline.

4. Service Management and Business.............................. 49

This essay continues with the conspectus of Service for academicians and practitioners. It follows the previous essay, entitled *Service Concepts and Facilities*, with the express purpose of defining the scope of the discipline. A thriving flexible service economy has emerged through globalization and digitization, and as a direct result, the modern enterprise has a dynamically changing boundary based on a portfolio of services obtained through make, buy, or rent decisions. Through the application of information and communications technology, many organizations have adjusted everyday operations enabling them to go through a transformational process to achieve revenue growth by being able to respond more quickly to changing market conditions and by being more effective and efficient in the application of services. The viewpoint taken here is that service management and modern business usually employ a complex computer infrastructure, but their domain is by no means restricted to computer-based services.

5. Service Technology and Architecture........................... 77

This essay concludes the conspectus of Service for academicians and practitioners. It follows the two previous papers, entitled *Service Concepts and Facilities* and *Service Management and Business*, with the express purpose of defining the scope of the discipline. An eclectic background in service technology and service architecture is required to fully explore the potential of a science as an academic discipline. This essay reviews the technical concepts needed to apply the concepts that have previously been introduced.

6. Service Principles 117

This essay delineates the principles of service systems, based on an ontological foundation of the subject matter developed independently of a particular endeavor, that are required to enable communication among researchers and assist in the ongoing theoretical development of the constituent topics. The essay begins with the presentation of service elements and progresses through the various topics until the requisite concepts, relations, and vocabulary are formulated. The subjects are presented in a developmental manner to promote clarity and readability for a broad service science audience and to support research in the discipline.

7. Service Design 141

This essay is a conspectus of service design. Historically, science has been concerned with the discovery and study of natural and socially developed phenomena, and the role of design has been to create new artifacts and processes and to improve existing ones. Service has been an important part of the fabric of societal culture from ancient times, so the notion of service as the co-creation of value by provider and client is well established. It necessarily follows that the objective of service design is to add value by enhancing the efficiency, effectiveness, and efficacy of older service systems and to create newer ones with requisite attributes. This is a topic that has not been covered in traditional service science research. Thus, service design, as a discipline, seeks to facilitate the operation of the modern global economy that is now based on service. The necessary elements of service design are introduced and important concepts are identified.

8. Service Innovation 167

This essay covers service innovation for service practitioners. The subject has not been accorded the attention it deserves, because of inadequate professional and academic attention to the subject of service, in general, and service design, in particular. The changing of one's perception of the human landscape from products to services is indeed cumbersome and entails a lot of effort on the part of the service establishment and the service entrepreneur. However, a new view of an age-old agenda in light of the ongoing move to globalization can be enlightening and rewarding. If Thomas Edison were engaged in services, he would have put it this way, "Service innovation is 90% perspiration and 10%

inspiration." Heretofore, innovation has been unfortunately aligned with the business community that has been distracted by an outdated and simplistic view of competitive advantage based on comparative economics. Effective service innovation is based on differential economics through service delivery that supplies better services as seen by the customer. Service innovation applies equally well, if not more so, to the other human endeavors of engineering, government, education, social services, political science, and a wide-range of unclassified interpersonal relations. The paper gives a modern view of service, innovation, service innovation, and how to unearth services innovation in a practical sense.

A service system is a socially constructed form of interaction wherein entities exchange beneficial forms of action through the combination of people and technology that are constantly adapting to the changing level of information in the system. Through the interaction of people, technology, and information in differing proportions, it has been conjectured that service systems exhibit the emergent properties of complex adaptive systems. This paper explores the relationship of service systems, complex adaptive systems, and social constructionism. This topic has not heretofore been treated in the service systems literature and should be regarded as an important component in the ongoing development of the science of service systems. The approach taken here identifies the service event as the underlying component of a complex adaptive system.

Business evolves according to market conditions, based on availability and choice. The purpose of this paper is to develop a model that describes how service provisioning evolves through a metaphor of selection, survival of the fittest, replication, and mutation. Clients are free to choose a service provider within a provider category, and the model describes and delineates that behavior. Equations and examples are given.

The *k*-**Factor** is the ratio of the value of intangible service to the value of tangible service. The ratio changes as a function of time and is an important cornerstone of modern business, because of our propensity for measurement and analysis. The concept applies to the traditional forms of service (people processing, possession processing, and information processing), as well as to Internet services and service-oriented architecture. This is a *working paper* on the *k*-Factor with the express purpose of extending the discipline of service science and providing a basis for further research.

In the area of service, a methodology is needed to distinguish one service from another and to define classes of services. A DNA of services is proposed consisting of a service DNA sequence of five letters corresponding to a five-dimensional quadrant-based scale. Each type of service is assigned a DNA sequence. If two services have the same DNA sequence, then they are in the same service class. The methodology provides a basis for classifying services, service models, and service systems.

Government has a major effect on the lives of most persons and the operation of almost all organizations. It would appear that there is general acceptance of the fact that government is in reality a service and that the voting public should have some voice in the service provided. However, that is where the agreement ends. If government is a service, then who is the provider and who is the client? Does the government provide services that are paid for through our taxes, or on the other hand, do we provide services in order to support the government's own agendas – possibly unknown to the general public. If government is the provider, then do individuals (as clients) generally expect more than they should from their taxes? More specifically, should individuals expect less from and provide more to their government? On the other hand, should the taxpayers (as providers) support the collective intentions of government? Lastly, should the operation of government be held to the same standards as individuals? This paper addresses the above issues from a service perspective.

To Margaret

Preface

This is little book is a collection of essays written by the author on the subject of service. They all have been peer reviewed and prepared for a variety of reasons. Some essays have been written to suit a general audience, and others have been prepared for a select class of readers. There are some formatting differences due to the basic requirements of the varying circumstances.

The essays are designed to be read separately resulting in a minimal amount of definitional material being repeated. The reader is able to comfortably read the entries on a topic of interest and disregard the remainder. The essays are related, but each has a unique focus.

The subject matter can be viewed as three separate sections: introductory, foundational, and applicative. The introductory essays are straightforward and give a gentle introduction to what the discipline of service is all about. The foundational essays provide a basis for the study of the concepts and methods of the service discipline. The applicative essays are general in nature, so as to provide insight to what does and can go on in the world of service. Essays 1 and 2 fall into the first category. Essays 3, 4, and 5 are in the second category, and the remainder are in the third group.

The table of contents is unique in that the entries give an introduction to the respective essay. This is an aid to selection and gives a summary of the subject matter that is covered.

The essays were assembled to support two recent books on the subject of service[1]:

Introduction to Service: What It Is and What It Should Be
and
  Service Concepts for Management: A Practical Approach

---

[1] Both books were published by iUniverse in 2017.

Service and Service Science are new fields of study and learning. Unfortunately, insufficient time has elapsed for the development of a set of case studies suitable for that form of study. It is hoped that this collection will partially fill that void.

Harry Katzan, Jr.

1

A BRIEF VIEW OF SERVICE

Introduction

Academic studies and the popular press have identified myriad trends impacting today's business environment. Some of these trends are:

- Globalization
- Price competitiveness
- Advanced financial markets
- Proliferation of technology

The most common reactions to the trends have been to achieve product differentiation, enterprise responsiveness, and process efficiency by focusing on core competencies. Accordingly, many businesses have reorganized to leverage their human and software assets to more fully support the core processes and outsource other elements, thereby relying on service companies. Many of the service organizations specialize in information systems and call-center operations and are located off-shore.

The service sector dominates the U.S. gross national product and constitutes more than 80% of its economic output and employment and should also be given serious consideration.

Because services are so widespread in today's global economy, many leading organizations have expressed the need for a science of services.

Services

A *service* is a provider/client interaction that creates and captures value. A unique characteristic of service, unlike agriculture and manufacturing, is that both parties participate in the transaction, and in the process, both capture value. In a sense, the provider and the client co-produce the relationship. Agreements, specifying responsibilities and expectations, are required and in most cases, enhance the benefits to both participants.

It is useful to consider the differences between products and services. Products are tangible and services are intangible. Products are storable; services are non-storable. With products, consumption follows production. With services, consumption and production occur at the same time. As product classes mature, they become standardized and competition shifts to price. Services are almost always customized. In general, products are capital intensive, and services are labor intensive.

Clearly, the differences apply to personal services as well as to organizational services. The focus in this paper is on organizational dynamics that apply to business, government, and education. Three major topics are covered: the lifecycle model, service-oriented architecture, and web services.

Lifecycle Model

The theory of how firms evolve has been covered in detail by Cusumano, et al.[1]. In industries where dominant designs prevail, firms compete on product features. As the industry matures, the competition shifts to price. Finally, the emphasis shifts to services. In many cases, as product revenues decline, as is commonly the case, the firm is transformed into a services company.

Product decline is the result of a saturated market, wherein it is difficult to locate new customers. Strategic consulting and long-term maintenance contracts, as well as product customization, facilitate the transformation from product to service. Competition drives down prices and margins, but less so for services.

In this model, the distinction between products and services sometimes becomes blurred. A product is the primary offering of a company, and a service, when offered by a products company, is commonly a complementary activity. A service for one company may be a core offering for another.

In some industries, such as software products, products are preferred to services because product replication is a small expense. In others, such as enterprise applications, customization and installation are expected and services are tied to product sales.

Products and services are considered to be complementary assets, but the existence of a product tends to create the need for a service. Over time, there is a tendency for firms to supplement their service assets through service migration.

Service-Oriented Architecture

Service-oriented architecture refers to the remaking of the organization (taken here to mean the corporation, government, and education) through four key components:

- Strategy
- Process
- Workforce
- Technology

The integration of computing capacity, network connections, and open standards, have allowed formerly complex problems to be solved within the domain of the four components, such that IT is a co-producer rather than a cost-reducer or a productivity enhancer [2]. The integration of strategy, process, workforce, and technology is the central theme of service-oriented architecture, in the sense that organizations are offering services instead of products, but also using the architecture to manage themselves.

Through open standards, software is becoming componentized, so it can be delivered as a service over a network. How to do this is service-oriented architecture (SOA).

A key element in SOA is the *strategy framework*, consisting of the following approaches:

- A representation of an organization factored into well-defined components
- A framework to identify alignment decisions

- A software repository of business process models
- A means of evaluating service partnerships

The *process framework* reflects a continual business optimization governed by standards of best practice and key performance indicators. *Human capital management* (HCM) refers to the innovation necessary to create and maintain an agile, flexible, and adaptive workforce. HCM is necessary as boundaries between organizations become blurred through service arrangements and partnerships develop. *Business performance management* is linked to the SOA of the IT infrastructure and involves the modeling, deploying, monitoring, analyzing, adapting, and running of core activities.

Service-oriented architecture results in a shift to innovative breakthroughs rather than incremental improvements through the integration of computing, networks, and standards.

Web Services

A *web service* [3] represents architecture for creating applications that can be accessed from different computers over the Internet using XML messaging. Generally speaking, web services are considered to be a business-to-business (B2B) technology designed to support new business models. Organizations that have deployed web service technology are using the capabilities to assemble the best capabilities available in the marketplace.

A web service consists of a set of pre-packaged and tested software artifacts deployed by an IT organization to meet business commitments. Components are available for discovering and employing services through network protocols and informational resources. Key elements are a service registry, a service requester, and the service provider. A web service is dependent upon two key sets of standards: network and messaging. Network protocols satisfy the first requirement and XML the second.

Lastly, the web service management system requires a service-level agreement (SLA) to establish a relationship between a service and a business process.

Web services together with its sister concepts, namely the life-cycle model and service-oriented architecture, permit the remaking of the organization through what is generally know as "value nets" – covered next.

Value Nets

A *value net* [4] is a means of capturing business value from the integration of strategy, process, workforce, and technology. Business value is created by shifting from the traditional value-chain model to a value-net model.

In the value-chain model, an organization creates value by adding elements to the finished product at each stage of a production process. In a general sense, raw materials are converted to value in a step-by-step production line. The modern competitive environment, however, requires faster turnaround time and more choices.

Successful enterprises currently use value nets in which suppliers and business partners interoperate through information over networks on a demand basis. The relationships between organization, suppliers, business partners, and customers are dynamic and adjust to changing requirements. Value nets are efficient because of the real time combination of services supplied by the key participants – the business, buyers, suppliers, and business partners.

Future Work

Services are ubiquitous. Even so, three views of service science are presented: the evolution of services in the product lifecycle model, service-oriented architecture, and web services.

References

[1]   Cusumano, M, Kahl, S, and F. Suarez, "Product, Process, and Service: A New Industry Lifecycle Model," April 21, 2006, unpublished report.

[2]   IBM Research, "Services Science: A New Academic Discipline," 2006, unpublished report.

[3]   Gottschalk, K. Graham, S., Kreger, H., and J. Snell, "Introduction to Web services architecture," IBM Systems Journal, Vol. 41, No. 2, 2002.

[4]   Cherbakov, L., et al, "Impact of service orientation at the business level", IBM Systems Journal, Vol. 44, No. 4, 2005.

[5]   Katzan, H., "A Client's View of Service Systems," Mini Conference on Service Science, Decision Science Institute, Pittsburgh, PA, 2007.

[6]   Katzan, H., "A View of Services Science," Proceedings of the Southeast Decision Science Institute, Savannah, GA. 2007.

***** End of Essay 1 *****

2

A CLIENT'S VIEW OF THE QUALITY OF SERVICE

Introduction

Most persons think that they know what quality is – at least in everyday affairs. When a discussion finally gets to the factual stage, as it usually does, a determination of quality turns out to be more a state of mind than it is a delineation of particulars. In a manufacturing economy, particulars are in fact observable and quality is easily determined. In a service economy, quality turns out to be a social construct established by real or perceived values. Times are changing and so has the view of manufacturing quality. Vargo and Lusch [1] view goods as appliances for service delivery, such that "… all economies are service economies." Vargo and Lusch present a fresh look at service and service management from a marketing perspective.

Service And Service Systems

The concept of service has its roots in economic activity that Fitzsimmons and Fitzsimmons [2] classify as extractive, secondary, and services. *Extractive* refers to agriculture, mining, forestry, fishing, and so forth. *Secondary* refers to manufacturing and processing. *Services* refers to everything else, subdivided into domestic, trade and commerce, and personal. Most professionals would probably want to add information services to the latter category.

Services are usually classified by two mechanisms: degree of labor intensity and degree of customer interaction. Again most professionals would probably want to add the level of knowledge required by the service provider and the amount of information supplied by the client as part of the service bundle. Clearly, a client's perception of the service experience is directly related to the intangible value of the information provided.

In a ground breaking paper on the Science of Service Systems, Spohrer, et al. [3] give several characteristics of a service event: customer participation, simultaneity, perishability, intangibility, and heterogeneity. *Customer participation* refers to the co-production of the service experience, and *simultaneity* refers to the fact that services are produced and consumed simultaneously. *Perishability* refers to time perishable capacity from the provider's viewpoint and opportunity loss from the client's perspective. *Intangibility* normally denotes the obvious fact that goods are not produced by a service event, but that characteristic is misleading, since many of the service performed by government agencies and educational institutions are not-at-all services from the client's viewpoint, but are societal requirements. This is a topic that requires investigation. Lastly, *heterogeneity* refers to the variation in services from client to client and the recognition that a service system is a complex system and the client-provider interaction can be mediated by information technology.

Social Constructionism

Social constructionism, aka Social Constructivism, is the theory of knowledge based, at least in part, on the social and material setting in which a belief is produced or maintained.[4] In social constructionism, individuals and groups participate in their perceived reality, and create a branch of knowledge as espoused by the philosophical doctrine of Equal Validity.[5] Equal validity suggests the notion that other means of knowing exist in addition to the factual predominance of scientific validity. Consider three examples: baseball, a baseball bat, and a five-cent coin. None but the hardened skeptic would deny knowledge about the three examples is a valid form of knowledge. Clearly, baseball is a socially developed activity that has evolved into a non-trivial game of strategy. It is knowledge that is socially developed. Similarly, a baseball bat is constructed from wood that we as a society have discovered and would exist without the game of baseball and the social setting in which it exists. The precise form and substance of the bat is, however, a socially constructed form of knowledge. So it is with the five-cent coin that represents more in a social setting than its chemical elements.

Service systems are socially constructed forms of interaction wherein entities exchange beneficial forms of action through the combination of people and technologies that adapt to the changing level of information in the system.

As such, reality constructed through social mechanisms is a dynamic process re-produced and maintained by social interactions. When persons interact, as in the execution of a service event, their shared perceptions of reality are reinforced as part of an objective reality.

Service Is Clients

Many people believe that if you build a better product, people will buy it. Unfortunately, the same sentiment does not apply to services. Service is a time perishable capacity that cannot be stored, such that a lost opportunity is lost forever. Accordingly, yield management is a customary practice in services with seasonal variation. Since "the process is the product," however, there is clearly more to service systems than service management.

In order to confront the subject of service quality, it is first necessary to have clients. Two approaches have achieved notable acceptance: demand management and capacity management. *Demand management* includes the following practices:

- Reservations or appointments
- Price incentives
- De-marketing key periods

Similarly, *capacity management* incorporates the following ideas:

- Part-time employment
- Shift scheduling
- Self service
- Making customers wait

Lastly, clients have to be educated to be active participants in the service process. As the level of technology increases in the execution of a service event, the level of education would necessarily increase as well.

Service Is Client Interaction

The most visible form of service quality is the manner in which clients interact with their service providers. Traditional service events such as the doctor/patient relationship, service establishments (such as dry cleaning), telephone reservations, and so forth, are obvious. Technology related forms of interaction demand a set of ontological categories. One such set of categories divides the problem domain into face-to-face contact and face-to-screen contact as follows.

Face-to-Face Contact
Technology free
> Exemplified by personal and professional services

Technology assisted
> Only the service provider has access to technology, as in health care.

Technology facilitated
> Both client and provider have access to technology

Face-to-Screen Contact

Technology mediated
> Access services such as call centers, restaurant reservations, and hotel reservations

Technology generated
> Service provider is replaced with technology, such as ATMs, checkout scanning, airport kiosks, and web services

Client/provider interaction is the primary determiner of service quality.

Service Is Quality

Service quality is determined by a client's expectation of service and the client's perception of the service that is experienced [2]. Expectations are developed by word of mouth, personal needs, and past experience. The service that is delivered is a complex combination of reliability, responsiveness, assurance, empathy, and tangibles [6]. *Reliability* refers to the consistency of service. *Responsiveness* reflects the perception that the provider is willing to provide service. *Assurance* is a measure of the competence of the service provider. *Empathy* is a reflection of the personal attention afforded to clients. *Tangibles* refers to the infrastructure as it is related to the service experience. Certainly, the five attributes of service quality reflect a traditional setting and do not take into account the complications associated with technology driven service provisioning.

One of the primary considerations is the education of the client. With conventional business systems, most employees possess some degree of education in information systems and tacitly develop realistic expectations concerning service delivery. Accordingly, service delivery is usually highly regarded and deemed of high quality. In lesser developed business areas, the professionals are normally unfamiliar with information services and their method of delivery. Obvious examples are healthcare and biology research, in which many of the client personnel have unreasonable expectations based on services rendered to other areas. In many cases, client professionals are unable to relate their specific needs. Innovation based on the pull theory concept is necessary to supply client driven needs.

A related determinant of service quality is security in a networked operational environment [7]. Many modern computer applications utilize web services provided through some form of outsourcing. Service-oriented architecture provides the basis for wrapping legacy applications and providing their access along with modern web-driven applications. Are the web services secure? The challenges are manifold and necessarily relate to security goals as they relate to service provisioning. Appropriate service-level agreements are only part of the problem, since security threats are constantly changing. Clearly what are required are the delineation of security goals and an overall needs assessment, as they relate to threats, attacks, and the service definition.

Summary

An approach to the science of service systems based on social constructionism was presented. The social dimension is one of the primary determinants of service systems research. This approach has not been covered in the literature before and is less developed than many of the other areas of services research.

The vehicle for the paper is service quality, which is related to most areas of information technology and web services.

References

[1] Vargo, S. and B. Lusch, "Service-Dominant Logic Basics, "www.sdlogic.net, 2007.

[2] Fitzsimmons, J.A. and M.J. Fitzsimmons, *Service Management: Operations, Strategy, Information Technology*, New York: McGraw-Hill/Irwin, 2006.

[3 Sporer, J., Maglio, P.P., Bailey, J., and D. Gruhl, "Steps Toward a Science of Service Systems," IBM Research, Almaden Research Center, San Jose, CA, www.almaden.ibm.com/asr, 2007.

[4] "Social Constructionism," www.wikipedia.org, 2007.

[5] Boghossian, Paul A., *Fear of Knowledge: Against Relativism and Constructivism*, Oxford: Oxford University Press, 2006.

[6] Metters, R., King-Metters, K., Pullman, M., and S Walton, Successful Service Operations Management, Boston: Thomson Course Technology, 2006.

[7] Hollar, R. and R. Murphy, *Enterprise Web Services Security*, Boston: Charles River Media/Thomson Course Technology, 2006.

[8] Katzan, H., "A Client's View of the Quality of Service Systems," Mini Conference on Service Science, Decision Science Institute, Pittsburgh, PA, 2007.

***** End of Essay 2 *****

3

SERVICE CONCEPTS AND FACILITIES

HISTORICAL OVERVIEW

Recognizing that more than 80% of the country's GNP results from services and also that more than 80% of the workforce is employed in services, Sam Palmisano, CEO of IBM, initiated a corporate-wide program in Service Science that has transformed IBM and many other organizations. The cornerstone of the program is the fact that even though most of us are engaged in services, we really know very little about the subject. At the time, there was no academic subject called "service science," no principles of service science, no theorems, and most importantly, there was no set of best practices. He has changed all of that. An important aspect of the IBM initiative is that it has enabled academic participation in the development of the subject matter through the establishment of a field called **Service Science** in a similar manner to the way IBM assisted in the development of academic programs in Computer Science, three decades ago. Responding to this situation, the IBM Corporation initiated a project in the years 2004-2007 to develop a science of services. The project has resulted in tidal wave of activity within the business and university communities to study the subject and develop academic programs. With Service Science, we are interested in the underlying principles that define the subject matter and demonstrate its relationship to other disciplines.

Service Science has the potential to change the way we think about and subsequently view the new world order and may eventually change the predominant economic focus from products to services. Since services are the cornerstone of most modern businesses, there is a high level of interest in the subject by persons from business, government, and education. Major corporations have supported intellectual activity on the subject by giving introductory presentations at many conferences and by providing liberal access to relevant information on corporate Web sites. The subject of service science has been addressed in papers in most business and computer conferences, usually in the area of service management and service marketing because a clear description of exactly what constitutes service science has not heretofore been available.

SERVICE CONCEPTS

This section gives an overview of Service Science for academicians and practitioners with the express purpose of defining the scope of the discipline. Many of the basic concepts are commonly known or easily acquired – especially if a person thinks about them. Some of the concepts you just never think about.

Service

A *service* is generally regarded as work performed by one person or group that benefits another person or group. It is an activity and not an element of property. Another definition is that it is a type of business that provides assistance and expertise rather than a tangible product. Still another definition is that it is after-purchase support offered by a product manufacturer or retailer. In employment, it is work done for business as an occupation. We are going to refer to it as a provider/client interaction in which both parities participate and both parties obtain some benefit from the relationship. The provider and the client exchange information and adopt differing roles in the process. A service is a form of activity, consumed at the point of production.

Normally, an element of service is a *process* – or a diverse collection of activities – applicable in principle to business, education, government, and personal endeavors.

Service System

A *service system* is a socially constructed collection of service events in which participants exchange beneficial actions through a knowledge-based strategy that captures value from a provider-client relationship. The definition is based on the notion of a system, which is a group of interdependent components that form a coherent whole and operate together to achieve a purpose.

The inherent service strategy is a dynamic process that orchestrates (or coordinates) infrastructure, employees, partners, and clients in the co-production of value. Based on a theoretical framework for creating economies of coordination, research on service systems incorporates a detailed analysis of various and diverse service events, so as to develop a view of the service scape.

Service Science Abstraction

Service science is an abstraction of service systems in the same way that computer science is an abstraction of computer-based information systems. The procedure, in both cases, is to take a piece of an existing system and put it under the microscope of academic scrutiny. In this particular instance, we are taking a service centric view of enterprise systems and economic activity, where traditional enterprise functions are candidates for being packaged as enterprise services.

Service Characteristics

The concept of service has its roots in economic activities that are classified as extractive, secondary, and services. *Extractive* refers to agriculture, mining, forestry, fishing, and so forth. *Secondary* refers to manufacturing and processing. *Services* refer to everything else, usually subdivided into domestic, trade and commerce, information services, and personal. This is a very general definition intended for the reporting by the government of economic conditions. In order to get a handle on services, we need better definitions.

A *service* is a provider/client interaction that creates and captures value. A unique characteristic of services, unlike agriculture and manufacturing, is that both parties participate in the transaction, and in the process, both capture value. In a sense, the provider and the client co-produce the service event, because one can't do without the other. It stands to reason that the roles of the client and the provider are different. In a doctor/patient service event, for example, the physician brings knowledge, time, and the necessary infrastructure. The patient brings him or herself, a medical history, and a perceived situation that requires attention. During the service process, the participants exchange information in various forms, resulting in a change to the people involved. The doctor's experience level and assets change, as do the patient's information level and physical or mental condition. There is more to it, of course, but this is the basic idea.

Service and Organizations

For organizations, the case is slightly different. Some companies, such as professional firms, are totally service oriented. Other service companies, such as airlines and restaurants, have more complicated arrangements. An airline company, for example, could contract out its telephone reservation service to another company. This process is called *outsourcing*.

Continuing with the airline example, let's assume that an agreement is made with a company in another country to run a call center whereby passengers can make reservations and obtain information. The airline is the client and the call center company is the provider. How does the client (that is the airline company, in this case), who is a stakeholder with something to gain or lose, effectively control the situation? They collectively draw up a *service level agreement* that governs the quality of service, the number of calls to be handled in a specified period of time, the duration of the agreement, and the costs involved. Why don't the patient and the doctor have a service level agreement? They do, but it is implicit in the social setting in which medical services are performed. In many areas of service management, the key element is the service-level agreement.

In government, service is governed by convention and law. Constituents use governmental resources for information and a variety of physical services. In many cases, it is difficult to tell who is providing the service and who is receiving it. In education, the provider/client relationship can be complicated. Who is the provider and who is the client? Let's assume that the teacher provides the service to the student, by giving lectures and managing classroom activity. But it could be more complicated than that. Consider a university setting. Does the professor provide a service to the administration by teaching courses and doing the myriad of other things faculty do? But then again, one could look at it the other way around by contending that the purpose of the administration is to provide service to the faculty and students by supplying the educational infrastructure. So the teacher could be a provider of services and a client of services, at the same time.

Business Service

Some firms further complicate the picture by essentially being in two related service businesses at the same time. Consider an information technology (IT) company that provides services in two forms: consulting and outsourcing. With consulting, the firm tells a client how to do something, and with outsourcing, the firm does it for the client. As an example, the IT firm could advise on what information systems the client needs and then develop those systems. Similarly, it could provide information on how to set up an IT operation and then run that shop after it is set up.

Related to IT services is a general class of activities known as *business services*. With business services, like IT services, there are two options: consulting and outsourcing. With business service consulting, organizations are advised about business function, such as customer relationship management (CRM) and enterprise resource planning (ERP). With outsourcing, the business services firm does it for you – perhaps in the areas of finance and accounting.

What we have at this point are multiple organizations, collections of people and technology connected by value propositions and shared information, operating as a service system. More specifically, a *service system* can be viewed as a configuration of people and technology connected to another system of people and technology in order to co-create value for both organizations.

Differences between Products and Service

It is useful to consider the differences between products and services. Products are tangible and services are intangible An automobile, a garment, a table, and even a fast-food hamburger are examples of products. A doctor's visit, swimming pool cleaning, and package delivery are examples of services. On the surface, one could conclude that products are produced through some relevant sequence of operations, but that is not a defining characteristic, since most services also go through a sequence of steps. The answer is that a product is an artifact – something you can see or touch. Clearly, a service results in something worthwhile – otherwise, why engage in it – but the result is a change in a person or possession, not in the creation of something.

Products are storable; services are non-storable. You can store any of the examples of products, given above. If you have your car cleaned or your lawn mowed, you can't exactly save that service. When a service is finished, it is done forever. Perhaps, a record of the service is archived, explicitly or implicitly, but once the stop button is pushed, that service machine is off. If a service has to be repeated, then it is another service event.

Another related difference is that services are generally regarded as perishable. The implication here is that if a seat on an airline flight is not used, then the value of that opportunity is lost. There are many parallels between services and events in everyday life. If you buy a fresh banana and don't eat it within a reasonable time period, its value is lost. You can buy another, but again, that is a different thing. Product and services are two different things.

With products, consumption follows production. In fact, the build-store-sell and the sell-build-ship business models apply here. With services, consumption and production occur at the same time. This characteristic is related to the difference between product quality and service quality. With products, a quality assessment can be made before the customer enters the scene. With services, the client's view of quality is determined during the service process. As product classes mature, they become standardized and competition shifts to price. Services are almost always customized. In general, product development is capital intensive, and the delivery of services is labor intensive. It is important to recognize, however, that the creation of products may include services in the production process, and that services may also accompany production in the form of follow-on activity.

Classification of Services

Given that services are pervasive in modern economies, there would appear to be so much diversity between them that it would be impossible to make any sense of the subject. On the other hand, there has to be a set of common denominators that we could use to classify services so that we could draw some conclusions about organization, performance, and quality.

Services are generally classified by at least five criteria: service process, service nature, service delivery, service availability, and service demand. The major factor is a qualitative concept, known as "service nature" that consists of service object and service result. We will focus on the service object, because it reflects whether a service is performed on a person, a possession, or information. In a previous section, we covered the subject of distinguishing services from goods. The service object is useful for distinguishing services from services, and it preserves the roles of the provider and the client. In a generic sense, the question of who or what gets the service is the determining factor in exactly how much of the other four criteria are applied to a particular service event.

People Processing Service

In people processing services, the provider performs corporeal actions to the client. The client is part of the service production process and remains in the domain of the provider during service delivery. There is simultaneity of production with consumption in a people processing service event, and the provider and client, are regarded as co-producing the service. Various forms of transportation service, for example, are placed in this category.

Possession Processing Service

In possession processing services, the provider changes the state of one or more tangible objects under the jurisdiction of the client. Many possession processing services are straightforward, as in car washing and other maintenance activities. These services relate to the condition of an object and are regarded as physical services. Clearly, there are other attributes of service objects and one of the most common is ownership that puts retailing into the domain of service processing. In fact, some manufacturing operations consist of a sequence of services applied to a physical object or system. Another physical attribute is location, and an operation that provides components to a just-in-time production process is a form of service. Package delivery, for example, is a form of possession processing.

Information Processing Service

Information processing services deal with the collection, manipulation, interpretation, and transmission of data to create value for the client. Accounting, banking, consulting, education, insurance, legal, and news are commonly experienced examples of information processing services. There are important issues with information processing services, such as representation (as with lawyers and accountants), infrastructure (as with computers, databases, and the Internet), and self service (as with online facilities, ATM machines, and other administrative functions).

Characteristics of Services

In spite of the prevalence of services in everyday life, the subject is rarely considered and seldom defined. In business, services are commonly referred to as the non-material equivalent of a good. Services can be sold, purchased, and scheduled. To many people, a service represents something they cannot do themselves or do not want to do, or perhaps more importantly, something that can be done more efficiently or in a less costly manner by a specialized business entity. Here are some characteristics of services:

A service is a process. This notion is paramount to recognizing the far-reaching importance of service science as an academic discipline. A service takes input and produces output. In between the input and the output, there exist one or more steps that constitute the service process.

A service is heterogeneous. This characteristic reflects the fact that each client/provider interaction in the form of a service event is unique.

A service captures value. A service event creates a benefit to both the client and the provider, in the form of a change of state that is reflected in their physical condition or location, a change in their possessions, or in their assets.

A service cannot be inventoried. The notion of opportunity loss is fundamental to service science. An empty seat on an airline flight cannot be resold. The value lost to a service provider due to a missed appointment cannot be regained. This characteristic gives a time dimension to services. Thus, a service capacity is said to be *perishable*, referring to the fact that it is "perished" when unused.

A service is intangible. A service event does not produce a physical product as a result; however, a service can produce a noticeable result.

A service is consumed at the point of production. This characteristic adds specificity to the recognition that a service is a process, even though it may be summarized for descriptive purposes as a service event. When a service terminates, it is finished. After the final step in a service process, the event is archived along with the consequent change of states of the client and provider.

A service cannot be resold or given away. It is not possible to pass a service on to another economic entity. The result of a service event is unique to that event, although information gained during the service process could theoretically be used by another entity. However, information resulting from a service event is not the same as the service event, because of the consumption characteristic.

A service is co-produced. This characteristic emphasizes the fact that because of the simultaneity of client and provider participation and the fact that a service event does not result in the production of a good, but rather in the state of something, it is commonly referred to as the co-production of value in the sense that if either of the participants were not present for the service event, it could not be interpreted as being a service.

Service characteristics are useful for distinguishing one service event from another and for defining classes of services.

SERVICE SYSTEM CONCEPTS

A *service system* is a collection of resources and economic entities, capable of engaging in or supporting one or more service events. The resources are the infrastructure and other facilities necessary to support the service process. The economic entities are the service provider and service client that co-produce the service event. In the case of possession processing services, the service environment would also consist of one or more tangible objects that serve as the service object of the service process. In most cases, a service system is required to sustain a service event. A service system consisting of a provider, a client, and a service target is conceptualized. In this instance, the service target could be the client, a possession of the client, or an individual or an organizational entity over which the client has responsibility.

Service Facilities

If a service provider and client can co-produce a service event, there must be some degree of geographical locality to the situation, in the sense that the client travels to the provider or the provider travels to the client or the client and provider execute the service event in a third-party location or they communicate via some form of interactive device and its corresponding media. In other words, they have to get together.

> **The Service Factory.** Let's first consider the case where the customer travels to facilities associated with the provider, such as an airline terminal, hospital, restaurant, retail establishment, or hotel – to name only a few examples. We will refer to the provider facilities, in this case, as the *service factory*. The basic idea is that the customer remains at the service factory during service delivery. The situation quickly gets complicated because it depends on whether or not the service is associated with a tangible object, an intangible object, or a production supply chain. A *pure service* is a service not associated with tangible objects, such as in medical treatment, hair coloring, and personal transportation. The service event is scheduled, initiated, terminated, and archived – all in the service factory. Many service processes are comprised of several steps called the *service chain*. Other services, not just pure services, consist of a service chain, but this characteristic is normally associated with pure services. When a service process consists of a service chain, it is said to be "scripted." Clearly, a service script may be implicit in the service, such as a doctor's visit, or it may be explicitly prescribed as part of a formal service agreement. Depending upon the complexity of the situation, services can

also be a part of a goods production process or a conventional supply chain. A related consideration is whether the service is classified as being discrete or continuous. A *discrete service* takes place in s short time interval – such as hours. A *continuous* service takes place over a longer period of time – such as days or longer. Moreover, a continuous service may be comprised of several service events, as in insurance or banking. Hospital service is continuous consisting of a series of service events. Moreover, the service events may be dynamic in the sense that they are not necessarily planned beforehand. A doctor's visit, on the other hand, ordinarily consists of a service chain of planned events, wherein the services might include check in, get weighed, interact with the physician, and so forth. Some continuous services, such as insurance and banking, incorporate a service factory that is closely associated with the provider but not the client. Clearly, services of this type have a service initiation, service steps, and eventually a termination; but in-between service events are dynamic in the sense that they may occur on an unscheduled and unplanned basis. Still other services in this category may utilize more than one service facility, such as a check-in terminal and a transportation vehicle. However, the classification applies since the client occupies provider facilities for the duration of the service. Branch banking is a form of continuous service with more than one service facility.

The Service Shop. Some services involve leaving a possession of the client at a service shop for later pick-up, as in the cases of dry cleaning and auto repair. Clearly, the service shop is associated with the service provider, and the service object, owned by the client, occupies physical space in the service facility for the duration of the service process. Child day care, for example, would be placed in this category.

The Service Portal. Other services engage a virtual service facility for the duration of the service event. All of this sounds like the Internet, and that's the idea. However, the category also includes telecommuting and a variety of online and telephone services. In fact, any activity, generally classed as e-Commerce, falls under the umbrella of a service portal. Included in the category of service portals are a variety of information services and "do it yourself" activities.

Mobile Service Facilities. In the previous categories, the emphasis has been on provider resources that occupy a fixed space, incorporating personnel, buildings, equipment, machines, vehicles, and supplies. The scenario has been that the client travels to the service facility or accesses it via some modern convenience. In other cases, the client moves as in navigation services and various forms of satellite communication, such as radio, information providing, and related services – such as car unlocking.

Client Facilities. The subject of service provisioning would not be complete without the mention of client facilities, as in the case where the service provider travels to the client to perform a service. In most instances in this group, the service is performed on a possession of the client – even though that is not a necessary condition.

Service Implementation

All organizations and all persons do not have the same service requirements and accordingly, the same problems. Moreover, it is impossible to look at services from solely an industry perspective or even a personal point of view. Clearly, services differ between industries and between persons. On the other hand, the diverse set of activities, universally called *services,* wouldn't be called *services* if there weren't some degree of commonality among them. Accordingly, we are going to take a look at steps in the service process, not necessarily service interactions, per se, that are commonly incorporated into the service chain. Service *initiation* refers to the steps necessary to schedule a service and establish a provider/client interaction. Appointments with professional service providers are normally scheduled, whereas arrangements with nonprofessionals are commonly scheduled on an informal basis. Some service providers use appointments to manage demand as a means of achieving service efficiency. Entry service *administration* initiates customer input, such as filling out forms, and establishes a service agreement encompassing fees and expectations. Legal documents may be involved with this step, and client requirements are delineated. Service *interactions* are the steps in the service process. For discrete service processes, service interactions are statically planned with expected variations, since most services are customized by the provider for each client. For continuous service processes, service interactions are dynamically engaged – as in the case of banking, insurance, and hospital care. Service *termination* represents the end of a set of service interactions, regardless if they are statically or dynamically executed. Follow-on services or referrals are established during this step. Exit service *administration* initiates the record-keeping process and deals with the economic aspects of the service process. Service *archiving* handles information storage and legal requirements.

Collectively, the six generic functions are normally present, explicitly or implicitly, in practically all service processes, and are referred to as the *service platform*. The intended meaning of the terminology is that the service platform supports the service process.

Business Service Systems

The basis of business service systems is the evolution from collaboration to automation. The first phase, entitled *Collaboration*, utilizes human engineering principles and is characterized as "assistance by doing some of the work." The next phase, entitled *Augmentation*, utilizes technology to increase productivity by using tools to supplement human activity. The third phase, entitled *Delegation*, is the outsourcing to service providers of non-core business processes that do not provide competitive advantage. The final phase, entitled *Automation*, employs technology to provide self-service systems. Employing the four elements of business service systems, namely organization, technology, management, and information systems, service businesses can move among the phases by considering the following elements: business value (*Should we?*), technology (*Can we?*), governance (*May we?*), and business priorities (*Will we?*).

Globalization

A business service system is a complex socio-techno-economic system that combines people, technology, value, and clients along four dimensions:

information sharing, work sharing, risk sharing, and goods sharing. There is some evidence that some elements of all four dimensions are present in all business service systems. Before globalization, services were performed between provider and client with some degree of locality. After Globalization Three, business value creation through services is created by sharing. Information and communications technology (ICT) is the key business driver in value creation and is the form of technology most closely aligned with business service systems.

Outsourcing

Outsourcing is the transfer of the ownership of a business process to a supplier, which includes management and day-to-day execution of that function. The most commonly outsourced business processes are information technology, human resources, accounting, customer support, and call center operations. The key characteristics of outsourcing are "transfer" and ownership; it is different from the process in which the buyer retains control and tells the supplier how to do the work. The objective of outsourcing can be and often is one of the following: reducing costs, focusing the capability of a particular business on more profitable activities, and to obtain special capabilities that the provider firm may possess. Core business competencies are usually not outsourced. For example, airlines commonly outsource telephone reservation and information systems to foreign companies in order to reduce costs and focus on flight operations. Another example, more close to home, is the outsourcing of business cleaning services to benefit from economies of scale for that type of service.

With outsourcing, the client and the provider enter into a business relationship, established with a substantial business agreement, and then the service provider takes over the business process. Outsourcing is usually – actually, almost always – associated with offshoring, but that need not necessarily be the case.

Offshoring

Offshoring is a general term that describes the relocation of a business process from one country to another. Although the present context is services, the practice also applies to manufacturing and production. If a country can provide services in a less expensive manner than other countries, it gives them a comparative advantage to freely trade those services. In the modern world of ICT for the appropriate services, therefore, offshoring can be achieved by establishing the necessary business ecosystem.

To be more specific, offshoring is the practice of transferring an internal business process of a company in one country to another country, to be executed by the same or a different company. Service offshoring is particularly appealing to modern business since many services can be digitized thereby facilitating inter-country relocation.

Offshoring may involve the transfer of intellectual property and training to the receiving country and is related to the availability of educated and trained labor as factors in production – the others being land and capital. Accordingly, many design and development services are being redirected offshore.

Outsourcing and Offshoring

It follows from the above discussion that a company that engages in the transfer of an entire business function to another company in another country is both outsourcing and offshoring. As mentioned previously, common examples of outsourcing are call centers, accounting, customer support, human relations, and information technology (IT). It is now appropriate to add medical diagnosis, design services, and engineering services to the list and recognize that both outsourcing and offshoring are involved.

Public opinion on combined outsourcing and offshoring (O&O) is negative, because it is generally felt that the process adversely affects individuals and the total labor market. Even in cases in which O&O is associated with lower jobless rates, it is felt that O&O tends to shift displaced workers into lower paying jobs.

Transformational Outsourcing

Many executives feel that outsourcing allows the firm to concentrate on core competencies and, in the case of ICT, achieve greater flexibility. Because many business processes are totally dependent upon computers, business agility is necessary for developing responsiveness in the marketplace. *Transformational outsourcing* refers to the combination of cost saving with the potential for strategic flexibility and supplements cost focus with opportunity focus.

The underlying idea is that through transformational outsourcing, the firm will be transformed into one with the requisite characteristics. Innovation in supplying services is required, therefore, because services are almost always customized and are labor intensive. Moreover, competition in the services marketplace does not tend to drive down process and profit margins. The key point, of course, is that outsourced services do not usually provide differentiation in the marketplace.

Sharing

The major tenet of services is that the provider and the client co-produce a service event and the composite interaction creates value for both of the participants. To a greater or lesser degree, a service is enacted by sharing, as covered previously. Information sharing is more closely aligned with services in which persons interact, such as medical provisioning and consulting. Work sharing is characterized by outsourcing. Risk sharing (although not covered so far) is associated with continuous form of service, such as insurance, and is related to transformational outsourcing. Goods sharing is involved with certain formal tangible people-oriented services, such as hotel and auto rental.

Service Process Organization

Practically everyone has heard of or experienced service providers that traditionally have clients backed up with very long waiting times. A common example is the "not so fast" fast-food restaurant. In the world of services, organization is everything. While it is literally impossible to solve all service problems in a few pages, it is feasible to deliver an organizational design that is relevant to most service systems. A definition of a service system is:

A *service system* is a system of people and technology that adapts to the changing value of information in the system. It is important to emphasize that the "changing value of information" also refers to the service process itself. So it should be expected that a particular service organization would adjust to changing conditions in the workplace.

In the production of goods, a measure of organization is the level of inventory, even though the management of inventory can be a subject in its own right. With services, capacity is a key element, and long waiting lines are evidence of insufficient service capacity, ineffective demand management, or inadequate organization. In this section, a working model of service organization is presented that should serve as a starting point for looking at organizational issues.

An Example – Retailing and Services

The importance of service organization is inherent in retailing. Retailing is a service, as covered previously, and the sales service event changes the ownership attribute of a product. A significant aspect of retailing exists, however, that is associated with service organization.

There is a component in retailing that is directly related to the level of expected service as a function of the price of the product. Most customers possess a nominal price for a given product. If the sales price is lower than nominal value, then less service is expected. If the sales price is higher than the nominal price, then more service is expected or the product is deemed overpriced. Buyer behavior, therefore, is governed by a combination of price and retail service, so that buyer behavior is influenced to some degree by service organization.

INFORMATION SERVICE CONCEPTS

Through information and communications technology, modern society has made enormous advances in how we live and work. How far we have progressed is summarized by Microsoft chairman Bill Gates in a recent email message. "The ability to access and share information instantly and communicate in ways that transcend the boundaries of time and distance has given rise to an era of unprecedented productivity and innovation that has created new economic opportunities for hundreds of millions of people around the world and paved the way for global growth that is unparalleled in human history."

An *information service* is a resource capable of supporting a service event or instantiating a service event based on information. In other words, an information service can assist in the execution of a service, such as in retailing, or it can actually be the service as when buying a pair of shoes on the Internet – actually, the World Wide Web, but that distinction is not required at this point. The resource is a service provider that can take the form of a person or a computer. The execution of an information service event requires a service client that can also take the form of a person or computer, and the provider and client must interact in order to co-produce the service. The execution of a service event changes the state of the provider and the client, but a tangible object is not produced. An information service is commonly associated with computer technology, but that is not a necessary condition. The most definitive characteristic of an information service is that the information travels, which gives rise to new models of information management and communications technology.

A Personal Dimension

Most of the information that is communicated between people is about something. Clearly, there is some form of informational interchange that accompanies practically all services. Information service is more than the incidental exchange of information.

With information services, the client specifically requests information and the provider supplies it using some form of communications channel. The service request may be implicit in some other form of activity or it may be "ordered" on a demand basis, but it is nevertheless requested.

Data versus Information

Each provider/client interaction in an information service requires a context, and here is why. Pure unadulterated facts are known as *data*. *Information* is data in a particular context so it has a specific meaning. When you request some information about a subject from an Internet web site, for example, the context is supplied in some manner, such as from the site itself, the nature of the query, or even information in a previously requested web page. The context effectively gives meaning to data and turns it into information. The bits that flow through wires or through the air as electromagnetic radiation are nothing more than data, at best. Accordingly, it would be proper to say that it is an *information service* that turns a bunch of bits into something useful, such as a news story or downloaded music.

Ordinary Mail

Not all information services necessarily require a computer. The United States Postal Service is a case in point, as is its international equivalent, known as the PTT (Post, Telephone, and Telegraph), which do not require a computer in their basic form. Electronic mail (email as we generally know it) is also an information service, and it does require a computer. Each element has a sender and an intended recipient. Who is the service provider? It is certainly not the sender or recipient. Clearly, it is the mail service itself. The mail serves as the communications channel between the sender and the recipient. In most other information services, the communications channel is only a channel for communication and nothing more. With mail service, pickup, transportation, and delivery would appear to be the service, and the informational content of the message is not brought into the analysis.

Is Software a Service?

Yes. Software would appear to be a service, such as in document preparation and as suggested by the example of ordinary mail. Information is moved from one place to another and perhaps it is transformed a bit in the process. In document preparation, or word processing, as it is usually called, information is moved from an origin, such as a person's brain, through the nervous system, the person's fingers, and the keyboard to the computer and software and then to a document file. Nevertheless, it is transferred from one place to another. If electronic mail is considered to be a service, then it would seem that word processing is also. Consider another example. If you go to a tax preparation agency to have your return prepared, you consider it to be a service. If you buy a program for a small fee that does the same work as the tax agency, does it perform a service? Most people would agree that tax software is a service. In the same vein, presentation, spreadsheet, and database software would also be regarded as services.

There is another aspect to all of this, as exemplified by the word processing and email examples. The provider and client participate in the exchange of information, even though they may not be, and probably won't be, in close proximity. Thus, the distance metric is not necessarily significant in word processing, and in the case of email, even the time metric is also not significant.

Is *all* software a service? Perhaps, that should have been the original question. It is an open item. It is easy to conceptualize that office software for document preparation, presentation, graphics, data management, and data analysis could be regarded as services, since that software facilitates the transfer of information from one place to another. In the area of information systems, DSS (Decision Support System) software, for example, provides timely information to managers to aid in decision making. DSS software is definitely a service. What about AI (Artificial Intelligence) software, such as software that monitors gauges in a nuclear reactor? Then, if something goes wrong, the computer program shuts the reactor down before a meltdown occurs. Again, most people, especially those that work in nuclear power plants, would agree that it is a service. The debate could go on. For this paper, at least, software is a service.

Practically speaking, a software package, by itself, does not qualify to be an information service. In order to be functioning as a service, software must be operating on a computer in order to respond to a client's request in an appropriate manner. You always need a computer and communications infrastructure to support software services.

Enterprise Information Services

Information is the cornerstone of modern business, and government as well, and is the major ingredient in everyday commerce. In the study of information services, the distinction between information and the system to handle the information is often blurred. In this section, we will establish the difference between information and services.

A lot of information is about things: about a product or service, about travel arrangements, about how to do something, about an event, about a person or group, about something that has happened in the past, and so forth. We are going to refer to this type of information as *operand information*, and we are additionally going to refer to information that is involved with the service process itself as *operant information*. When the focus of an information service is the result, then as Vargo and Lusch might put it, we are using goods-dominant logic and the result is referred to as the operand. When the focus of an information service is on the process, then we are employing service-dominant logic and the operant resources are the information and the other steps in the service process.

Business Information

Business information services are usually divided into two categories: operational services and management services. Operational services are employed to run the enterprise and management services are used to manage the enterprise. Some of the same basic concepts are used in both categories, but the time and distance characteristics are different. For example, a database management system and a database are normally used to store persistent data for the enterprise. With operational services, the database is dynamic and is updated for each transaction. With management services, static data is needed to make effective decisions. Accordingly, a static database would ordinarily be created from the dynamic database so that timely management reports could be generated. Of course, this is a bit of a simplification, but the basic idea is there.

The management of information is an enterprise service in its own right. Clearly, the transfer of information from operational databases to a data warehouse is a concrete example of an enterprise information service.

Transaction Services

When you make an airline reservation or check a flight schedule using the Internet, you are using a transaction processing system. Most information services that support operational systems in today's world use transaction processing. At the most general level, you interact with the server using the communications channel. You are the client, the server is the provider, and the service is the transaction. The entire process is mediated by hardware and software and the only thing that moves is the information.

Client and Provider Input to an Information Service

An information service requires client and provider input, just as in any other kind of service. Usually, the client – whether it is a person or a computer – enters a small amount of information into the service process. The provider – usually a computer information system – has access to a larger store of information, so that we can say the provider provisionally supplies a larger amount of information. The informational output of an information service is a function of the inputs and the nature of the service.

The client may have help supplying input to an information service through hardware and software facilities known as "interaction services." The provider may have assistance from database services and auxiliary services via a service bus.

Interaction Services

An interaction service is normally a socially-constructed collection of structural elements and behavioral patterns, such as action buttons, list boxes, and pull-down menus. Interaction services are dependent upon what the client expects to do with the information service. Here are some examples:

- Information exploration (e.g., find out about service science)
- Accomplish something (e.g., reserve a seat)
- Find a "good enough" answer to a question (e.g., how do we get to New York)
- Change the direction of a search operation (e.g., what about service systems)
- Establish a point of reference (e.g., mark my place to come back to at a later time)

Designing effective interaction services is not so easy, but one approach is to think about the elements with which you have to work. A common set of such elements is composed of objects (such as icons), actions (such as a file menu), subject (such as the information that you have to work with), and tools (such as calendars and appointments).

Interaction services are a small part of service science, but nevertheless an important part.

Service Bus

A *service bus* is a high-speed data link between two computing platforms that operate in a request/response mode. The client requests an item of information (such as the price of IBM stock on Monday at 11:00 on a given date) and the provider, which operates in a server mode, supplies it in an expeditious manner. A service bus requires software that is called *middleware*.

An example of the need for a service bus is inherent in the following example. A stock broker is on a line to a client who requests the price of IBM stock. The brokerage firm has a computer (the server) that gets an up-to-the-second feed from the stock exchange. There is a high speed link between the stock brokers and the server, and each broker has a specialized thick client interface. The broker enters the stock symbol for IBM into a text box and clicks a send button. The server responds in a fraction of a second with the requested price.

Collaboration

Teams are the accepted norm in the modern enterprise, and collaboration is the process by which they progress toward a common goal. With information services, collaboration between groups and individuals can be effected from geographically dispersed locations. In general, collaboration has a well-defined structure and set of operational procedures that employs any or all of four recursive information service modalities: email, instant messaging, interactive media, and specially designed collaborative software.

Collaboration operates at the intellectual level and often benefits from decentralization and varying degrees of academic and personal diversity. Collaboration is a unique form of service. The service provider in the information service modality is established through information and communications technology, and is an instance of where the "service is the service provider," because it allows the clients in a collaboration service to exchange meaningful information.

Collaboration requires at least two clients interacting in what is referred to as a *multi-client service*. A multi-client service is frequently leaderless and is known as a *virtual organization structure*. Traditional workflow where a document is passed between team members is a common form of collaboration.

Pull versus Push

It is perhaps a bit of an oversimplification, but "the manner in which you approach an information service determines what you get." The characteristics of the *pull model* are succinctly summarized in the following sentence. "Rather than 'push,' this new approach focuses on 'pull' – creating platforms that help people to mobilize appropriate resources when the need arises."

Push models are essentially scripted and thrive in stable environments with little uncertainty. Forecasting, as in demand forecasting, is key in push environments and allows high levels of efficiency to be developed in business processes. Most of modern business and governmental activity uses the push modality. A business pushes a product into the marketplace and people buy it. Push programs are top-down processes with the following steps: design, deploy, execute, monitor, and refine.

Pull models increase value creation for both clients and providers. For clients, "pull" activity expands the scope of available resources. For providers, pull systems expand the market for services. Pull platforms are associated with the following attributes: uncertain demand, emergent design, decentralized environment, loosely coupled modular construction of facilities, and on-demand service provisioning. Pull models are more amenable to uncertain business conditions.

From both the client's and the provider's perspectives, pull services focus on the following activities: find, select, purchase, deliver, and service. If all of this sounds familiar, it should be. It represents how you buy shoes on the Internet.

Enterprise Service Constituents

The seven constituents of an enterprise information service are providers, clients, messages, communications, information processing, persistent storage, and the user interface that collectively take into consideration the requisite technology including database facilities, email archives, protocols, business rules, operational procedures, and a variety of service interactions needed for enterprise applications. Since information, and not people, move in information services, this category of service is based on information and communications technology. It is important that when we discuss information services at the enterprise level, we are primarily concerned with functionality and not necessarily with computing platforms.

Information Service Model

Information service systems typically operate in a client/server mode, which means that the end user is the service client, the enterprise application running on a computing platform is the service provider, and the means of client and provider interaction is some form of communications channel. Typically, the client enters information into the system through a well-defined interface and the provider does something in return. Exactly what the provider does is of primary importance to the information service system.

There are at least three distinct possibilities:

- The provider accesses some form of persistent storage and returns selected information to the client.
- The provider performs some element of information processing and returns an indicator to the client that it was done.
- The client and the provider enter into an interactive dialog concerning specific informational elements and a supply chain operation is initiated to accomplish the corresponding enterprise operation.

As such, information service systems are instrumental in supporting daily activities. Typical enterprise applications are order processing, purchasing, accounting, inventory control, human resources, marketing and sales support, manufacturing, and various forms of service support including data collection and information management.

Scope of Electronic Information Services

It is possible to be more definitive about electronic information services. Three main constituents are identified: business, government, and the consumer. How the information services are related is important. B2C indicates business-to-consumer. B2B indicates business-to-business. G2B indicates government-to-business. C2C indicates consumer-to-consumer. G2G indicates government-to-government. G2C indicates government-to-consumer. In the symbols, the leftmost letter reflects the provider and the rightmost letter represents the client.

Electronic Commerce

Electronic commerce is an enterprise information service application supported by the Internet and the World Wide Web, and can be viewed as an opportunistic means of doing business with minimal cost. In short, the information services of the Internet and the Web are used to conduct business.

Electronic commerce is usually known as e-commerce or B2C for short. Conventional business establishments are referred to as "brick and mortar" facilities characterized by a shopping area in which customers can view products, and business personnel can conduct commerce. The equivalent in the digital world is an e-commerce web site where a consumer can conduct analogous functions. The service provider is the e-commerce web site and the customer is the client connected to the web site via the Internet. In this instance, the Internet is the communications channel. The service process is the set of interactions between the customer and one or more web sites that go through the following steps: find, select, purchase, deliver, and service.

Find is an Internet service process, which is usually a set of service interactions, to navigate to the desired Internet retailer. After the electronic retailer is chosen, the *select* and *purchase* services represent the online equivalent of the traditional processes of making a purchase. Purchasing involves payment that invokes a secure service designed for that specific purpose. *Deliver* is another service process initiated by the retailer for physically delivering the product to the consumer. *Service* is the Web enabled service process of providing customer support. Each of the steps in the B2C service process (i.e., find, select, purchase, deliver, and service) involves at least one service, so the entire process can be properly regarded as a *multiservice*, driven by a series of constituent information services.

B2C transactions are characterized by increased convenience, enhanced efficiency, additional buying choice, and lower prices, from the consumer's perspective, and by an increased return on retailing investment for the electronic retailer. An electronic retailer need not have a related "brick and mortar" facility, but that is often the case.

Electronic Business

Electronic business is the use of the Internet and the World Wide Web to conduct business operations, including intra-business and inter-business transactions. This is a broad category and ranges from relatively simple information services to obtain tacit business information from within a single organization to complex Web Services and REST web services.

Electronic business is usually known as e-business or B2B for short and has its roots in electronic data interchange (EDI) commonly used to exchange information on business operations within an organization, and between business partners, suppliers, and wholesalers. The use of the Internet for communications services reduces operational costs for computer networks and increases the value obtained from costs that are incurred.

The major advantage of B2B operations is that companies can utilize an information service known as the "B2B Electronic Marketplace," wherein they can buy and sell products and exchange information through a *virtual marketplace*. Not only can companies create supply chains, but they can create business partnerships in which one company can take advantage of information services of another company. The process, known as the *componentization of information services*, facilitates the creation of web services that allow the company to be a more responsive (to market and economic conditions) enterprise.

B2B is similar to B2C in one respect. Modern company operations require the purchase of certain *indirect materials*, typically referred to as MRO materials, where MRO stands for "maintenance, repair, and operations," and include such items as ball pens, repair parts, and office equipment. Through the B2B electronic marketplace, various companies can collectively achieve lower cost through *demand aggregation*. *Direct materials* are items used in production or retail operations as part of a company's core business. B2B operations can also be sustained through web services.

Electronic Marketplace

Information services, such as the electronic marketplace, permit companies to engage in B2B market operations in horizontal and vertical electronic marketplaces. In a *horizontal marketplace*, buyers and sellers can interact across many industries. Travel and financial services are common examples, because they are applicable to almost any type of business, such as the process industries (oil and gas) and conventional and electronic retailing.

In a *vertical marketplace*, buyers and sellers are in the same industry and primarily engage in information services that relate to direct material.

Electronic Government

Information services are a means of transforming the management and operations of government to be more responsive, efficient, and reliable in delivering services to the electorate – at all governmental levels, including federal, state, and local communities. The objective is to enhance informational facilities that already exist so they may properly be regarded as click and mortar," with the options of obtaining information and services via the Internet and World Wide Web while continuing to have a physical presence. Three flavors have been identified: Government to Business (G2B), Government to Consumer (G2C), and Government to Government (G2G). In the latter case, there are two possibilities: inter-government and intra-government. Inter-government refers to the vertical alignment of information services between governmental levels on the same initiative, such as the coordination of federal, state, and local agencies on air pollution. Intra-government refers to the horizontal alignment of services between agencies at the same level of government, such as disaster response coordination between police, fire, and emergency medical departments.

Government to business operations reflect information services that cover purchasing of MRO materials, and the provisioning of information facilities for procedures, regulations, reporting, and compliance. In the latter case, governmental reporting facilities (by business to government) are commonly available to submit requisite documentation through Internet and World Wide Web services.

Most citizens are familiar with Government to consumer information services for taxes and various forms of registration. For taxpayers, the ability to download forms and directions, and the ability to submit completed tax forms is paramount. For those of us fortunate enough to receive a tax refund, the increased efficiency is money in the bank. Vehicle and voter registration are other information services that are efficient from both client and provider perspectives.

Overall, however, the availability of information on dates, procedures, directions, and so forth, at the click of a mouse via the Internet and the World Wide Web – pure information services – is the greatest advantage of G2C services.

PERSONAL INFORMATION SERVICES

Personal information services are an ever expanding collection of Internet and World Wide Web applications. The prevalence of the applications, however, brings up a fundamental question about exactly what constitutes the clients, providers, and the services in the various forms of information service. The resources appear to be different among the applications, so the presentation of the subject matter will be instructive for determining the scope of personal information services. Accordingly, we will cover the following services: chat rooms, instant messaging, Internet telephone, web auctions, user-generated media, social networking, and newsgroups. This is only a sample of relevant applications but is indicative of how information services are used to support those applications.

Chat Rooms

One of the most popular means of communicating on the Internet is through a chat room, the best known of which is IRC (Internet Relay Chat). IRC operates in the client/server mode and requires an IRC server; clients require special IRC software, usually downloaded from the Internet.

When using chat, the user selects a channel, which establishes the conversation in which the user will participate. Characteristically, other users, throughout the world, will have chosen the same channel. The idea being that they will exchange information on a certain subject.

During operation, users type messages on their local client computer and the information is relayed via the Internet to the server. The message is then forwarded to other users signed on to the same channel and is displayed on their screens. A user may just listen, figuratively speaking, or may participate in the conversation. Ostensibly, users respond to other user's transmissions, so that an identifying name (sometimes called a *handle*) accompanies each submission. Since chat rooms are a global phenomenon, a network of IRC servers is required to service all of the users in a specific domain. A recent development is "voice chat," which is an audio equivalent to the traditional text-based chat.

At the end-user level, a chat room can be viewed as a collection of clients whose interpersonal communications is being managed by the chat server system operating as a service provider. The chat server system consists of the hardware, software, and Internet facilities, necessary to do the task. The service process consists of a set of dynamically determined client/server interactions, where the end-user is the client and the chat server is the service provider.

Instant Messaging

Instant messaging is the private real-time communication of textual messages between two users logged on to an instant messaging (IM) server over the Internet. Messages are forwarded through an IM server that uses the "sender" client's buddy list to determine the destination for forwarded messages. Many Internet specialists consider instant messaging to be a form of chat room operations, since it has similar information service characteristics.

Front and Back Stages

Internet chat and instant messaging, among other information services, incorporate a value chain of component services, divided between front and back stages. Essentially, the front stage is what the end-user conceptualizes and the back stage is what is going on under the covers, so to speak.

The noteworthy aspect of the division is that human clients are only part of the process, if they are involved at all, and the front stage represents the client's experience supplemented by the back stage that represents the information service support structure based on ICT facilities. The participants (Human or ICT) may possess different but complementary views of the service process.

Internet Telephone

Using the Internet for making telephone calls is appealing to many people because of the cost, which may be free in some cases, over and above the cost of the Internet connection. Several methods and associated software facilities are available. They generally fall into two broad categories.

In the first case, you use special hardware and software to communicate through your personal computer (PC) using a microphone and speakers. If you are calling someone who is also using the same method, the call is totally free, as it is with web browsing and email, and it is also applicable to users anywhere in the world.

In the second case, you use your ordinary "land line" telephone handset, and the call is routed over the Internet using a service process generally known as Voice over IP (VoIP). With VoIP, your voice is digitized and routed through the Internet as information packets, similar to other information services such as web pages and email. At the receiving end, the voice packets are converted to normal telephone signals.

With Internet telephone, the conceptualized front and back stages coincide. The clients are the telephone users and the service provider is the value chain of Internet activities.

Web Auctions

A *web auction* is an Internet and World Wide Web service that connects buyers and sellers in a consumer-to-consumer (C2C) mode to conduct an online version of traditional auction. A well-known web site that manages the web auction process is *eBay*, but there are notably other sites that perform the same service.

In this instance, the information service is the posting and delivery of information concerning products for sale and associated bids. The clients are the buyers and sellers and the information service consists of the information processing facilities to sustain the auction. In this instance, the Internet and the World Wide Web serve only as a communication channel.

User Generated Media

There are three major forms of information dissemination normally originating from individuals that use the Internet and World Wide Web services: web logs, podcasts, and RSS feeds. The services are related and are covered together in this section.

A *web log* (called a *blog*) is a medium for presenting information without restrictions or review over the Internet and accessible through the World Wide Web. People who participate in the service of creating information content in this category are known as *bloggers*, and the process itself is known as *blogging*.

The following three information services are normally associated with this form of activity: (1) Obtaining information on how to set up and access a blog web site; (2) Providing services that assist in actually setting up a blog web site; and (3) Using services that assist in making entries in a web log. Each blog site has a uniform resource locator (URL) and a theme, subsequently used for search and discovery.

A *podcast* is an audio blog, serviced by the Internet that serves the same purpose as a personal radio station. Using your PC and a microphone, you can record a document and store it on an appropriate blog site. Other users can then download the audio blog to their PC for listening or for transfer to a music player. Podcasts are used to listen to broadcast media and educational material. In the latter category, a podcast is an effective means of delivering course material to students.

An *RSS feed* is a means of generating a wider audience for blogs and podcasts, through an Internet technique known as Really Simple Syndication. RSS feeds utilize special web formatted material and deliver automatically generated downloads to registered end users using push technology.

User-generated media operations are generally considered to be a front stage process. All communications are *asynchronous*, which means they are created (or uploaded) as a process at one time and accessed (or downloaded) by another process at another time, using push technology.

Social Networking

Social networking is usually regarded as the process of keeping up with friends and family, and it is no surprise that the process has migrated to the World Wide Web. The inherent information service is social networking is known as "shared space."

A *shared space* is an online virtual public space in which a person – commonly a young person – can display information about themselves, including text, audio, and video. Special web sites, such as MySpace and Facebook, are designed to handle social networking. Actually, the video is predominantly photographs taken with a digital camera and uploaded to an appropriate web site set up for social networking. A person's virtual space is subsequently accessible by friends. The conceptual model for a shared space is that of a private room to which one can invite friends to look around, thus giving the owner a private virtual space not otherwise available in everyday life. As with information services that support media, social networking services are asynchronous and use pull technology.

Newsgroups

A *newsgroup* is a collection of people that participate in a discussion on a particular subject using Internet facilities. The usual form of communication is email, and the mode of communication is question and answer. The largest and most widely known online news group is *usenet*. A participant subscribes to a particular topic. When that participant logs on to the newsgroup server, the entries on the selected topic are automatically sent to that participant. Special client software is required to participate in a newsgroup. User interactions are organized by thread, so that a given user effectively engages in a conversation, as required, with participants in the same interest group. If a thread is *moderated*, questions are sent to a human moderator who screens the questions for appropriateness. Otherwise, questions are simply listed by topic. Most threads are archived by date.

Newsgroup software employs the same information service modality as email, and in fact, is dependent upon email for its operational infrastructure. Newsgroup facilities are also available through most information service portals, such as America Online and Google.

QUICK SUMMARY

1. The subject of services is important to most people because they are employed in services and are also consumers of services. In the year 2000, U.S. service employment comprised 80% of the workforce. Surprisingly, very little attention is given to the service sector, in spite of the fact that most of us work in it.

2. A *service* is a provider/client interaction that creates and captures value. A unique characteristic of services, unlike agriculture and manufacturing, is that both parties participate in the transaction, and in the process, both capture value. In a sense, the provider and the client co-produce the service event, because one can't do without the other.

3. There are several definitive characteristics of services. They are summarized as follows. A service is a process. A service is heterogeneous. A service captures value. A service cannot be inventoried. A service is intangible. A service is consumed at the point of production. A service cannot be resold or given away. And finally, a service is co-produced.

4. A service system is a system of people and technology that adapts to the changing value of knowledge in the system. The participants in a service system are the provider and client and the relationship between them is the service process. Systems of this type require an environment in which to operate that can take the form of a service factory in which the client resides for the duration of the service process and the service shop in which a possession of the client resides for the duration of the service event.

5. Service systems are facilitated by information and communications technology and enhanced by globalization. Service provisioning is inherent in outsourcing and offshoring. Innovation in supplying services is required because services are usually customized and labor intensive.

6. Core business processes are not customarily outsourced, and outsourcing predominantly does not provide differentiation in the marketplace.

7. An *information service* is a resource capable of supporting a service event or instantiating in a service event based on information. In other words, an information service can assist in the execution of a service, such as in retailing, or it can actually be the service as when buying a pair of shoes on the Internet.

8. Most of the information that is communicated between people is about something. With information services, the client requests information and the provider supplies it using some form of communications channel.

9. Software would appear to be a service, such as in document preparation and as suggested by the example of ordinary mail. Information is moved from one placed to another and perhaps it is transformed a bit in the process.

10. Information is the cornerstone of modern business, and government as well, and is the major ingredient in everyday commerce. Business information services are usually divided into two categories: operational services and management services.

11. Operational services are employed to run the enterprise and management services are used to manage the enterprise.

12. Teams are the accepted norm in the modern enterprise, and collaboration is the process by which they progress toward a common goal. With information services, collaboration between groups and individuals can be effected from geographically dispersed locations.

13. Major enterprise information service applications are electronic commerce, electronic business, and electronic government. Major personal information service applications are chat rooms, instant messaging, Internet telephone, web auctions, web logs, podcasts, RSS feeds, social networking, and newsgroups.

REFERENCES

[1] Friedman, T.L. (2006), *The World is Flat: A Brief History of the Twenty-First Century*, New York: Farrar, Straus and Giraux.

[2[Gralla, P. (2004), *How the Internet Works*, Indianapolis, IN: Que Publishing.

[3] Hagel, J. and J. Brown (2007), *From Push to Pull: Emerging Models for Mobilizing Resources*, www.edgeperspectives.com.

[4] IBM Almaden Services Research (2006), *Service Science, Management, and* Engineering (SSME): *Challenges, Frameworks, and Call for Participation*, http://almaden.ibm.com/ssme, p. 13.

[5] IBM Almaden Services Research (2006), *SSME: What are services?* http://almaden.ibm.com/ssme.

[6] Katzan, H. (2008), "Foundations of Service Science: Concepts and Facilities," *Journal of Service Science*, *1*(1), 1-22.

[7] Katzan, H. (2008), *Service Science: Concepts, Technology, Management*, New York: iUniverse, Inc.

[8] Maglio, P. (2007), *Service Science, Management, and* Engineering (SSME): *An Interdisciplinary Approach to Service Innovation*, IBM Almaden Research Center, http://almaden.ibm.com/ssme, p. 14.

[9] Maglio, P. and J. Spohrer (2007), *Fundamentals of Service Science*, IBM Almaden Research Center.

[10] *Offshoring* (2007), http://en.wikipedia.org/wiki/Offshoring.

[11]   *Ontology* (2007), http://en.wikipedia.org/wiki/Ontology.

[12]   *Outsourcing* (2007), http://en.wikipedia.org/wiki/Outsourcing.

[13]   Richardson, L. and S. Ruby (2007), *RESTful Web Services*, Sebastopol, DA; O'Reilly Media, Inc.

[14]   Spohrer, J. Maglio, P., Bailey, J. and D. Gruhl (2007), *Steps Toward a Science of Service Systems*, IBM Almaden Research Center, San Jose, CA, www.almaden.ibm.com/asr, 2007.

[15]   Spohrer, J., Vargo, S.C., Caswell, N., and P.P. Maglio (2007), *The Service System is the Basic Abstraction of Service Science*, IBM Research, Almaden Research Center, San Jose, CA, www.almaden.ibm.com/asr.

[16]   Stair, R.M. and G.W. Reynolds (2008), *Principles of Information Systems: A Managerial Approach*, Boston: Thomson Course Technology.

[17]   Tabas, L. (2007), *Designing for Service Systems*, UCB iSchool Report 2007-008, February, 2007.

[18]   Tapscott, D. and A.D. Williams (2006), *Wikinomics: How Mass Collaboration Changes Everything*, New York: Penguin Group, Inc.

[19]   Tidwell, J. (2006), *Designing Interfaces*, Sebastopol, CA: O'Reilly Media, Inc.

[20]   Vargo, S. and B. Lusch (2004), "Evolving to a New Dominant Logic for Marketing," *Journal of Marketing*, 69 (January, 2004), 1-17.

[21]   Vargo, S. and B. Lusch (2007), *Service-Dominant Logic Basics*, www.sdlogic.net.

***** End of Essay 3 *****

4

SERVICE MANAGEMENT AND BUSINESS

ENTERPRISE SERVICE CONCEPTS

In the multifaceted domain of services, management and business are intertwined. An enterprise, taken in this paper to be a business, government entity, or educational organization, simultaneously manages its own services and services provided to clients by adopting the role of service provider or service client. In short, an enterprise is likely to be a provider and a user of services. In fact, many internal services are managed as a business and in some instances evolve into external service providers – all with the same or similar functional deployments. So the fine line of separation between management and business is nonexistent, and that phenomenon is clearly evident in the following sections. Any conceptual overlapping of the subject tends to enforce the contention that the two subjects support each other.

SERVICE MANAGEMENT

Historically, the focus of service management has been on the application of traditional management concepts to enterprise processes that primarily involve services. Typical business examples are banking and health care that have greatly benefited from the application of scientific principles to everyday operations. Two common applications are the use of waiting-line methods for the front office and process scheduling techniques for the back office. Through the application of information and communications technology (ICT), many organizations have adjusted everyday operations enabling them to go through a transformational process to achieve revenue growth by being able to respond more quickly to changing market conditions and by being more effective and efficient in the application of services. This section describes modern services management. The viewpoint taken here is that services management employs computer concepts, but its domain is by no means restricted to computer-based services and includes just about any service that a person can imagine.

Service Management Concepts

There are three forces operating in the sphere of service processes. The first is the use of ICT enablement in providing revenue growth, efficiency, and effectiveness for traditional and enhanced services, as well as for conventional business processes. This subject is commonly referred to as information systems. The second is the consulting services domain that provides IT services to external organizations. The third is the use of ICT to manage information systems and services, which is a field of endeavor known as IT Services Management. Briefly said, it is the use of computers to manage the enterprise and also to manage itself.

Domain of Service Management

Many people feel that what you see in the world depends on the lens through which you are looking. So if you adopt a service-centric point of view, most socially-developed phenomena can be viewed as services. It follows that if we are going to manage services, we should at least consider to whom services are applied and how the service delivery is achieved.

We are going to focus on an organizational setting consisting of people and everyday operational units. The *service provider*, in this instance, is a person acting in a service capacity or a group of persons, including support facilities, that has adopted a role of a service provider. The *service object* is another person or operational unit, usually referred to as a *business unit*. In the latter case, the service object need not be part of the same organization as the service provider. Some examples of service relationships are: (1) an accounting department in a manufacturing company; (2) a computer support person in an academic department; (3) a consulting group that services external customers; (4) an IT department that serves several business units in the same organization; and of course (5) a service professional serving several clients.

There are at least three different types of service arrangements:

Type I: The service provider delivers services to only one service object.

Type II: The service provider delivers services to more than one service object in the same organization.

Type III: The service provider delivers services to one or more service objects in external organizations.

Once a provider type is identified, in a particular instance, the next step is to determine who pays for the service and specifically how that support is organized. This process is known as *service provisioning*.

The internal processes of effective service management go through a cyclic process, known as the *service lifecycle* that includes service strategy, service design, service transition, service operation, and continual service improvement. The use of the methodology presented in this section is known as *best practices*. Most service organizations and all IT organizations would perform better if they adopted a set of best practices, and clearly, many of them do.

Service as a Business

The notion of service has its origin in ancient times and was understood to mean "one person doing something for another." With the advent of civilization and industrialization, the definition of service was implicitly extended to encompass "one person doing something for an organization," usually in the form of employment. At this stage, specialization and entrepreneurship kicked in with all of their rights and privileges resulting in what we now recognize as the service organization.

Specialization has its roots in process efficiency, but has definite social overtones. Some jobs are more lucrative and have more prestige, and for a variety of reasons, people can do some tasks better than others. Specialization is not limited to individuals but applies to organizations and groups within organizations, as well. Specialization is commonplace, not only in service organizations. In conventional business processes, such as a sales group, certain tasks are performed more expeditiously by a single individual or group, as with credit checking, when the task is performed repeatedly. The degree of specialization needed in a service process is related to the amount of repeatability. Most production and service chains divide the process into individual tasks that are performed by a single unit, taken here to be a person, group, or machine, such that efficiency and effectiveness is achieved through specialization.

Innovation flourishes in a receptive service environment, so that effective service groups are commonly at odds with their parent organization. Service spin offs have resulted in a thriving service economy through entrepreneurship and innovation. Accordingly, it is important to recognize that *service is a business*, and that the principles given here apply equally well to internal and external service organizations.

Service Componentization

Services are ubiquitous, so practically everyone knows what one is. Well, maybe they can't exactly define it, but they recognize one when they see or experience it. What most people don't think about, unless they have to, is that a service is a process. Beneath the surface, there is usually a collection of activities to support that process. The activities are organized into components.

A *component* is an organizational entity for instantiating services. Some components provide more than one service and some services are comprised of more that one component. The operation of a simple restaurant is used to clarify the concept of componentization. (Adapted from Hurwitz, Bloor, Baroudi, and Kaufman (2007).)

> We go to a restaurant for a meal. The meal is the service we are seeking. We grab a table, look at the menu, and give our order to a waiter or waitress. Subsequently, the meal is delivered. We consume the meal, pay the tab, and leave. In our interaction with the waiter or waitress, we exchange information, so in a very general sense, we co-produce the service event, although we do not experience the meal preparation. This is not a pure service, since the food is a product. However, the service part of the meal is a service.

On the other hand, we all know that the restaurant is a collection of interacting components that provide a meal service to one or more guests. The components of the restaurant are the server (i.e., the waiter or waitress), the kitchen (that prepares the food), a cleaning component, a food-ordering component, an accounting component, a facility-management component, and a restaurant management component that orchestrates the services supplied by the components. The *service orchestration*, which is an explicit or implicit specification of the interactions between components, is a necessary element in the design of a managed service system.

Collectively, the arrangements of components that make up a service offering constitute its architecture. In service architecture, some components are internal persons or units, some components are outsourced, and some components are business partners. One aspect of service management is the choreography of components in a specific business process – that is, how information or tasks are passed between components without explicit direction.

Another important aspect of service management is keeping track of the components and their attributes. When a service organization gets complicated, a service repository is required to keep track of the services that are provided by each component, and what components are needed for a particular service process. Usually, a computer database is used. From a strategic viewpoint, a component is an asset that must be managed just as any other asset.

IT Services Sourcing

There are several aspects of IT services that can vary between organizations. Examples are commonplace: computer operations, network management, hardware and software acquisition, system analysis and design, software design, software development, information systems integration, and call center and help desk operation and management. This is a representative set of tasks necessary for sustaining an IT services organization. You can do them yourself; you can have another business entity help you do them; or you can have a business entity do them for you. In the latter two cases, the business process is known as *IT service outsourcing*.

Most IT services reflect an underlying set of IT assets, such as hardware, software, users, and systems. The IT services organization has three possible roles regarding these assets: develop or acquire, operate, and manage. For each of the IT assets, role adoption can differ. For example, hardware can be acquired internally and operated by an outside contractor.

The entity that provides the service, that is, the external business unit, need not be an independent business entity in a foreign country. It can be a separate business unit in the same enterprise, located locally, in the same country, or offshore. Alternately, it can be an independent professional services business entity in the same country – a service usually regarded as *IT consulting*. In many cases, however, the organization providing the outsourced service *is*, in fact, an independent business entity operating out of and located in a foreign country.

IT Services Management

It would seem that a person's view of IT services management would be different, depending on whether your organization is the service provider or the service client, and indeed, it is. The common denominator between the various perspectives is the set of common issues that business and IT managers have to deal with, some of which are strategic planning, IT and business alignment, measurement and analysis, costs and investment, business partners and relationships, sourcing, continuous improvement, and governance. The issues are repetitive, recurring, and ongoing, and constitute a *service lifecycle*. The elements of the lifecycle are generic and do not necessarily apply to all service systems. Differences lie in the adoption and deployment of the lifecycle elements.

At the heart of IT services management is a set of tasks that involve "keeping track of things," and there are a lot of things to keep track of. We will call them *service elements*. Some of the service elements are obvious, such as users, hardware, software, network components, office facilities, and configurations. There are other service elements, mostly related to enterprise operations that can offer a challenge, such as categorization of services, to whom those services are supplied or alternately, from whom those services are obtained – contractors, outsourced projects, outsourcers, and business partners. A *service directory* is needed for this type of record keeping. Lastly, with regard to business alignment and service operations, there is a whole host of service operational elements that collectively possess business value that should not be ignored. Three of many such service operational elements are incident management, problem management, and change management. It is through the integration of service operational elements that an enterprise can achieve significant business value. The subject is covered in a later section.

Elements of the Service Lifecycle

The service lifecycle consists of five important elements, listed as follows: Service Strategy, Service Design, Service Transition, Service Operation, and Continuous Improvement. This sequence represents the waterfall model that suggests how the requirements process goes from strategy to continuous improvement, implementing a feedback process as required. Each element of the service lifecycle is considered separately.

Service Strategy

The most important element in the service lifecycle is service strategy. Successful service operations are not sustainable over long periods, because of environmental turbulence affecting resources, competition, and requirements. Accordingly, a service strategy is needed. A *strategy* is a long term plan, based on objectives, that allows an organization to adapt to changing conditions.

Since service is a client based endeavor, it is necessary that a service delivers perceptible value. A service strategy based on client needs is necessary for successful service operations. A service strategy, recorded in s *strategy document*, should reflect whether the strategy is intended for a provider or a client. How an organization uses a service strategy is an individual matter. A service document should reflect major items, such as whether services are managed internally or outsourced, who the key collaborators are, and what service management functions, such as problem and incident management functions, are needed.

Service Design

Service design refers to the synthesis of services to satisfy enterprise objectives. This stage has general applicability, even though it appears, on the surface to reflect IT services. Service design incorporates service architecture, processes, policies, and requisite documentation. Even though the service strategy phase identifies services, the service design phase is where they are established to satisfy business objectives. Even though a computer-based service is developed offshore, it is usually developed by the parent organization during this phase. Risks, quality, measurement, and infrastructure requirements are specified in this stage. Also, this stage involves capacity management, availability management, security management, and key organizational responsibilities.

Service Transition

Service transition concerns the implementation of services in the sense of putting them into a production environment. As such, service transition is an organizational bridge between the design and the operations stages. In many instances, the service transition phase involves a change to existing services involving limited functionality and operational procedures. As such, a service transition requires the establishing of or adhering to a formal policy for the implementation of required changes and the development of a framework for the integration of the changes. When additional training and help desk support is needed, it is established in the service transition stage, which may also include system validation and testing.

Service Operation

The function of the service operation stage is to manage and deliver the services established in the design stage. Business value to the enterprise is delivered in the operation phase, and event monitoring is of prime importance. A *service event* is a change of state during the delivery of a service that requires attention, such as an unplanned interruption of service. Two service management functions are commonly involved: incident management and problem management. *Incident management* is primarily concerned with resolving the situation and getting the system back up and running. *Problem management* focuses on determining the root cause of an event and interfaces with change management to insure that the problem is not a recurrent event.

Continuous Improvement

Continuous improvement, or more properly, *Continuous Service Improvement*, refers to the process of maintaining value to the enterprise of a service or set of services. Practically all enterprises, subscribing to services, engage in continuous improvement to some degree, to protect their investment. The output of continuous improvement, known as *Service Reporting*, feeds back into the other four stages, on an as needed basis, constituting the service lifecycle.

This stage consists of seven steps, listed as follows:

1. *Define what you should measure*
2. *Define what you can measure*
3. *Gather the data*
4. *Process the data*
5. *Analyze the data*
6. *Report the information*
7. *Implement corrective action*

Continuous improvement is an excellent management tool as it suggests a means of prioritizing ongoing strategy and design activities.

EVOLUTION OF SERVICE MANAGEMENT

This section covers three topics relevant to effective service management: value nets, the pull model, and E-services. The subject of service management is constantly evolving, because the modern enterprise has a dynamically changing boundary based on a diverse portfolio of services.

Value Nets

A *value net* is a means of capturing business value from the integration of strategy, process, workforce, and technology. Business value is created by shifting from the traditional value-chain model to the value-net model in service systems. In the value-chain model, an organization creates value by adding elements to the finished product at each stage of a production process. In a general sense, raw materials are converted to value in a step-by-step production line. The modern competitive environment, however, requires faster turnaround time and more choices, especially with regard to service management.

Successful enterprises currently use value nets, in which suppliers and business partners interoperate through information over networks on a demand basis. The relationships between organization, suppliers, business partners, and customers are dynamic and adjust to changing requirements. Value nets are efficient because of the real time combination of services supplied by the key participants – the business, buyers, suppliers, and business partners.

The Pull Model for Service Agility

Hagel and Brown have identified the pull model as a means of mobilizing business resources for the upcoming generation of business activities based on mass communications and the Internet. The characteristics of the *pull model* are succinctly summarized in the following sentence from the Hagel/Brown web report. "Rather than 'push,' this new approach focuses on 'pull' – creating platforms that help people to mobilize appropriate resources when the need arises." Push models are "script oriented" and thrive in stable environments with little uncertainty. Forecasting, as in demand forecasting, is key in push environments and allows high levels of efficiency to be developed in business processes. Pull models are more amenable to uncertain business conditions that require compressed development times for new goods and services. The pull model represents service architecture at the enterprise level, and could properly be viewed as *enterprise service architecture.*

The pull model is a profound concept, since most services are client initiated.

E-Services

Every year, businesses spend millions of dollars on their IT infrastructure, consisting of hardware, system software, applications, networks, people, and other organizational assets. With "on demand" computing, they can plug into the wall, figuratively, speaking, and only pay for the IT services they use. The concept is called *utility computing* that is accessed as are most public utilities. We are going to refer to the utility computing concept as *E-services*. An E-service utility is a viable option for the provisioning of computing services.

The concept of E-services is the packaging of computer services as a metered facility without up-front costs for IT infrastructure and is commonly used for large-scale computations or peak demands. In the current view of things, an E-services utility is network based and is dependent upon the Internet as a transport mechanism. In recent years, computing has become the operational medium for business, government, and education and part of everyday life for most people. As with electric utilities, computing utilities have evolved from being a luxury to an everyday necessity.

An E-service utility is characterized by four key factors: necessity, reliability, usability, and scalability. *Necessity* refers to the idea that a preponderance of users depend on the utility to satisfy everyday needs. *Reliability* refers to the expectation that the utility will be available when the user requires it. *Usability* refers to the requirement that the utility is easy and convenience to use – regardless of the complexity of the underlying infrastructure. *Scalability* refers to the fact that the utility has sufficient capacity to allow the users to experience the benefits of an expandable utility that provides economy of scale. Certainly, modern Internet facilities for search operations that engage thousands of servers satisfy these characteristics.

The notion of "paying for what one uses" is a compelling argument for using E-services for special or all computing needs. However, the proof of the pudding may, in fact, be in the details. The key question is whether the service should be based on a metered model or a subscription model. With the *metered model*, the usage is easily measured, monitored, and verified and lends itself to managerial control on the part of the user. In addition, metering can be applied to differing levels of service. With the *subscription model*, usage is difficult to control and monitor, and its adoption is favored by managers more concerned with convenience than with resource control.

For example, water and electricity service commonly use metered service while the plain ordinarily telephone system "usually" provides subscription service for local service and metered service for long distance. In the area of computer networks, broadband cable and telephone digital-subscriber line (DSL) rates are normally based on the subscription model. With cable TV, on the other hand, there are usually differing levels of subscription service along with "pay per view" for special services.

One can readily conceptualize a scheme for a typical E-service customer – nominally assumed to be a small-to-medium-sized business. Office services, such as word and spreadsheet processing, could be subscription-based service and special applications, such as integrated enterprise systems, would be metered service.

The difference between application services and multi-tenant services may very well be the deciding factor in determining whether metered or subscriber service is the way to go. With *multi-tenant service*, several clients may share the same software with separate data – as in the case of office processing. With *application service*, the service provider supplies one instance of the software per client, thereby lending itself to a form of metered service.

SERVICE BUSINESS CONCEPTS

Several important factors have contributed to the new business model based on services. The complexity of the modern work environment is perhaps the key factor, as well as the changing demands of a networked economy. The increased level of worldwide incomes has added to the desire for enhanced business and social services. The dependence on information and communications technology (ICT) has been an enabler of the complexity and growth of services by facilitating the connection between suppliers and consumers of services.

Business Model

A *business model* is a representation of a business, emphasizing its purpose, strategies, organization and operational practices, and capabilities. It typically covers the following: core capabilities, partner network, value proposition, customer base, distribution methods, cost structure, and revenue base. One of the functions of a business's organization and operational structures is to translate the business model into an objective reality.

The point of view taken here is that an operational service model is a business model.

Strategy and Mission

A *strategy* has been defined as "A long term plan of action designed to achieve a particular goal," and *governance* as "The set of processes, customs, policies, laws, and institutions affecting the way an endeavor is directed, administered, or controlled." The two subjects command our attention, because much of the economy and workforce are engaged in services; but, as we have alluded to before, we seem to know the least about what we do the most.

The basic tenet underlying strategy is that a principal entity desires to accomplish something worthwhile called a *mission*. A mission is required so the entity, be it a business, government agency, educational unit, or person, knows where it is going, and a strategy is needed so it knows how to get there. The mission is a service participant's goal, and the strategy is the roadmap for achieving that goal. A *strategy* is a plan of action.

Service Ecosystem Characteristics

Before the revolution in ICT services, the exchange of information was a supporting element in most aspects of economic activity. Through advanced technology, information is now an important component in the value proposition of most services.

The modern enterprise can now exploit informational resources on a demand basis from remote locations and without necessarily owning them. Moreover, the facilities necessary to sustain those resources may be shared, creating innovative opportunities for service provisioning.

Through web sites, mobile computing, and kiosks, self-service channels are currently available to support informational interchange. Business functions, such as billing, payments, ordering and order processing, reservations, online service support, and information management, are currently available without regard to time or distance.

Through innovation and entrepreneurship, new business opportunities are available on an on-demand basis, frequently constructed from existing services.

Strategic Assets

A *strategic asset* is a resource that provides the basis for core competencies, economic benefit, and competitive advantage, thereby enabling a service business to provide distinctive service in the marketplace. Because services are labor intensive, investments in people, processes, knowledge, and infrastructure are directly analogous to investments in resources for production and distribution in capital intensive businesses.

Strategic assets permit a service enterprise to achieve a competitive advantage through service differentiation, cost advantage, and superior customer response. *Service differentiation* involves providing a high degree of uniqueness in the service experience and also in the quality of service provided. *Cost advantage* refers to efficiency in the use of facilities, as in an airline terminal, and with 24/7 operations to maximize the use of infrastructure. *Customer response* involves flexible, reliable, and timely solutions to customer requirements.

Service Context

A *service context* supports the efficacy of service provisioning. The development of a service context involves the asking of tough questions to examine the strategic goal and objectives of a service organization in order to identify and establish a service portfolio. Here are some questions a service organization might want to ask of itself: (ITIL, p.9)

- What services should we offer?
- To whom should the services be offered?
- How do we achieve competitive advantage?
- What is our customer's value proposition?
- How do we establish value for our stakeholders?
- How do we define service quality?
- How do we allocate strategic assets to our service portfolios?
- What are the bottlenecks to growth and effective service provisioning?

The questions apply in differing degrees to whether services are provisioned for one organization (or department), one of more units within the same parent organization, or to units in different organizations. Moreover, the services apply within the following contexts: do them yourself, another business entity helps you do them, and have another business entity do them for you.

Service Perspective

Every reasonable business model demands a context, and the one presented here is no exception. Our service model is based on a service management concept for providing value to customers in the form of capabilities that translate resources into valuable services.

The objective of service provisioning – regardless of whether the service involves people processing, possession processing, or information processing – is to provide value to customers through an intrinsic knowledge of customer needs obtained by preparation, analysis, usage patterns, and the application of best practices. Within this perspective, a *service* may be alternately defined as a means of delivering value to customers by facilitating outcomes customers want to achieve without the ownership of specific costs and risks. (Clark. p. 5)

SERVICE FACTORS

Three factors determine the need for services and the realization of those services. They are: value, flexibility and control, and risk. With regard to the value factor, it is not just value, per se, but value versus cost. When costs are reduced through internal or external outsourcing, for example, there should be concern over whether the value of the service to the client is the same as or greater than before the outsourcing. Using resources and capability as inputs to a service, is the resulting value to the client commensurate with the cost? Similarly, when internal or external outsourcing is implemented, there is concern over operational flexibility and management control. Some organizations have experienced the "tail wagging the dog" syndrome and have had to bring major services, such as IT outsourcing, back into the parent organization. It is very difficult to modify strong service level agreements, so the parent organization is effectively constrained by the very services that were supposed to provide them with business agility. Also, successful outsourcing, in some instances, has been diluted through mergers and acquisition, whereby competing services have been assimilated into a parent organization, effectively comprising the original benefits. Lastly, there is risk inherent in relying on services, even though there is a customary risk to be expected in everyday affairs. The uncertainty in the application of service level agreements works contrary to the expectation on the part of clients to receive a positive effect with the utilization of assets.

Injecting a bit of reality into the analysis, there is always the headache factor. The possibility always exists that outsourcing or calling in a consultant, is a means of relieving an organizational headache – regardless of the cost.

Similarly, living with a third party in the form of outsourcing may be too much for some organizations to handle.

Service Creationism

In most views of service theory, there would appear to be service creationist forces at work. Through some unknown process, an enterprise comes to life and ostensibly needs service of some kind. (An *enterprise* for this discussion is a business organization, a governmental department or agency, an educational unit, or almost any other form of profit-or-non-profit socially constructed organization.)

A service organization enters the scene and identifies certain processes associated with the enterprise that it can use to make a profit. It's clear that the target enterprise is the service client, and the service organization is the service provider. The activity on the part of the provider that identifies candidate processes for the proposed benefit of the client is sometimes called service innovation. Usually, service innovation amounts to very little more than an elementary form of observational research. (At this point, we are only considering service innovation.) Product innovation involves other factors, although we can easily make the case that all products are actually services. In general, however, the tasks involved with creating and sustaining a service business usually constitute a rational process. The provider may possess superior capability, as is commonly the case with an IT consulting company that provides a variety of services to less experienced clients who choose to take advantage of the opportunity. The client's resources may be inadequate to effectively perform a particular set of tasks, as in the case of an enterprise that doesn't possess the needed people or technology to solve a particular problem or venture into a new area of endeavor. The client, in either of the cases, may choose to focus on core competency. In this instance, a core competency is a set of activities that affect the mission of the client. The use of services may be purely economic, which is usually the basis for most outsourcing.

Service creationism represents a provider–side view of service provisioning.

Service Evolutionism

On the other hand, a service evolutionist might view the subject of service acquisition in a different manner. With client-side service provisioning, the process of obtaining and deploying services evolves through several identifiable stages of organizational dynamics, based on the three factors presented above, namely value, flexibility, and risk.

Most enterprise processes are comprised of two kinds of activities: core functionality and supporting functionality. In a bank loan department, for example, the lending function is core, and credit checking is supporting. Similarly, in a pension writing department, the synthesis of a pension plan is core, and the back-office computer operations are supplementary. When multiple departments demand the same services, it is a common management decision to combine the service operations and in the process, possibly enhance the level of service. "Kick it up a notch" is the usual justification. This is the first stage, referred to here as the *service recognition stage.*

At this point the emphasis changes from operating a service to using a service on the part of the core departments. The core department is avoiding the risks and costs associated with the supplementary function, since service costs are shared. Let us call this the *risk/cost avoidance* stage.

After the need for non-core services is realized and instantiated, there is a universal tendency to reduce costs – because after all, the services are not core to the mission of the organization – or endeavor to make a profit on the service operation. A decision can be taken at this point to spin off the service department as a self-standing internal or external organization, or outsource the total operation to an outside service firm. It would appear that this is either the *spin off stage* or the *outsource stage,* as the case may be.

There are additional considerations, based on infrastructure and management control. Here are some options:

- Outsource the total operation, including infrastructure, people, and management control
- Retain infrastructure and management control and outsource the people and operations
- Retain infrastructure, management control, and operations and outsource the people
- Outsource certain tasks within any of the above options

Task-oriented outsourcing is perhaps the end game in the relationship between enterprise dynamics and service science. It is commonplace in modern business to have professional and technical tasks, such as engineering, software

development, and design, outsourced to specialist firms in much the same way that architectural services have existed for many years.

Service evolutionism represents a client–side view of service provisioning.

SERVICE UNDERPINNINGS

A *service business* is a collection of organizational assets that provide value to clients in the form of services by exploiting inherent capability on two levels: the client level and the provider level. Effective service provisioning permits the client to focus on core competencies.

Value Creation

The value of a service is determined by a client's expectation of service and the client's perception of the service that is experienced. Expectations are developed by word of mouth, personal needs, and past experience. The service that is delivered is a complex combination of five attributes: reliability, responsiveness, assurance, empathy, and tangibles. *Reliability* refers to the consistency of service. *Responsiveness* reflects the perception that the provider is willing to provide service. *Assurance* is a measure of the competence of the service provider. *Empathy* is a reflection of the personal attention afforded to clients. *Tangibles* refers to the infrastructure as it is related to the service experience. The five attributes of service quality reflect a traditional setting and do not take into account the complications associated with technology driven service provisioning.

To this important list, we are going to add availability, capacity, continuity, and security.

Availability, Capacity, Continuity, Security, and Risk

Availability reflects the degree to which services are available for use by clients under terms and conditions agreed upon in a service-level agreement. Clearly, a service is available only if the client can take advantage of it. Accessibility and expectations are major considerations from the user's perspective. The method of access should be made explicit in the service-level agreement and the user's expectations should be managed by the client. (The use of the terms *client* and *user* is intentional. Using the principal/agent model, the client is the principal and the user is the agent.)

Capacity is the ability of the service and the service provider to support the requisite level of business activity of the client. Demand for service must be available within a specified range and the service provider must be able to supply service provisioning during peak periods in a shared environment.

Continuity refers to the ability on the part of the service provider to support capacity during disruptive and catastrophic events. Continued service is not the only consideration. Alternate and backup facilities in the form of services must be in the service landscape.

Security refers to controls to assure that client assets will be safe from intrusion, disclosure, and physical destruction. Security refers to operational security *and* to the physical safeguard of client assets.

Availability, capacity, continuity, and security collectively determine the client's risk in acquiring services and assist in differentiating between service providers. When comparing the cost and value of services, risk should be factored into the equation.

Service Assets

Engaging in a business service would appear to be quite straightforward on the surface, but is actually a complex arrangement of business units, service units, services that connect the two, and provider types. The abstract term *business units* refers to the provider assets that give value to the client when applied. Similarly, *service assets* refer to the functions that the provider can perform. It follows that a *business service* is a mapping between the provider and the client, in much the same way that we ordinarily conceptualize the physician/patient relationship.

Service Portfolio

A *service portfolio* is a conceptual collection or list of services. Use of the term is intended to be analogous to a financial portfolio of investment instruments. However, there are major differences depending upon the *raison d'etre* of the portfolio.

A financial portfolio is ordinarily thought to be a collection of assets synthesized so that when the value of one asset goes down, another goes up. This is a bit of a simplification, but it's the idea that counts. The best case is when the value of all of the assets goes up, and the worst case is when the value of all of the assets goes down. Normal life is somewhere in between. With a service portfolio, there shouldn't be a downside, but some service firms do some things better than others.

With services, the *raison d'etre* of the portfolio depends on whether you are talking to a provider or a client. A provider portfolio might be a simple list of services – something an accounting firm might have as part of their marketing collateral. An IT consulting business, for example, could list items such as strategy formulation, service programming, and operations management.

From the client perspective, however, a service portfolio in indispensable, because it provides a central source of services agreed to in conjunction with the service provider, along with terms, conditions, and service metrics. A related concern is a database of potential suppliers of services.

SERVICE OPERATIONS FRAMEWORK

An *operations framework* is a set of service management functions (SMFs) established as best practices that assist in providing business value to a client. They should be organized and staffed by internal and external providers involved in IT-based or non-IT-based service operations. The service functions definitely have an IT flavor to them but apply to all provisioning in the services domain. Collectively, the SMFs agree with the ITIL compendium of best practices. ITIL stands for Information Technology Infrastructure Library. It is a set of best practices for IT Services Management (ITSM). Each of the generic SMFs is briefly summarized.

Service-Level Management

A service-level agreement (SLA) is a formal and signed agreement between the service provider organization and the business unit to document expectations and requirements of a service delivered to the business unit from the service provider. The agreement aligns business needs with delivery of services and facilitates delivery of solutions to business requirements at acceptable cost. It involves a definition of requirements, an agreement on specifications, operations management expectations, and a review clause. The tasks include the creation of a service catalog, the development of internal procedures, the ability to monitor and respond to operational conditions, and the ability to perform regular service-level reviews. The service catalog delineates the priority of service-level tasks, the expected effect on employees, a description of users, a listing and description of service assets, and the organization's business partners and suppliers. Service-level monitoring is a key issue. The major service metrics are availability, responsiveness, performance, integrity and accuracy, and security incidents. In order to perform the service-level monitoring, the following steps are required: the identification and criteria for monitoring, establishing thresholds, the definition of alert, the specification of alert management, and essential response definition.

Service-level determination and management is the key element in a service package.

Availability Management

Availability management is the service management function that insures that a given service consistently and effectively delivers the level of support required by the customer. Continuity of service is the key objective. The usual risks to availability relate to technology, business processes, operational procedures, and human error. Countermeasures that have proven to improve availability are testing of business processes, effective release procedures, and employee training. The areas most affected by availability issues are the implementation of new IT services, critical business functions, supplier behavior, and internal organizational factors, such as policies, procedures, and tools.

Capacity Management

Capacity management is the service management function that optimizes the capability of the service infrastructure and supporting organization to deliver the required level of customer service in the established time domain. Capability of service is the key objective. This SMF is most affected by people, infrastructure, and technology.

Service-Desk Management

The service desk ia a single point of contact for customers and service technicians with the intent of delivering responsive solutions to service needs. The major service desk functions are to handle single incidents and individual service requests. Service desk scheduling has historically been a concern, and the current trend is to have self-managed teams that utilize service triads or peak period scheduling. A *triad* consists of a three person team, with two people on and one off at any time.

Incident Management

The objective of incident management is to detect events that disrupt or prevent execution of critical or normal IT services, and to respond to those events with methods of restoring normal services as quickly as possible. An *incident* is any event that is not part of the standard operation of a business process that causes, or may cause, an interruption to, or reduction in, the quality of service. In this context, a *problem* is the root cause of an incident; a *solution* is a method for resolving an incident or problem that resolves the underlying cause; and a *workaround* is a means of restoring a specific incident without resolving the underlying cause.

Problem Management

The objective of problem management is to investigate and analyze the root causes of incidents and initiate changes to service assets to resolve the underlying problem. The key function of problem management is to reduce the impact of incidents, problems, and errors on the organization by applying methods of root cause and trend analysis.

Change Management

The objective of change management is to provide a formal process for introducing changes to the service environment with a minimal amount of disruption to normal service operations while insuring the integrity of critical business functions. Change management preferably goes through several distinct steps: change initiation, change request, change classification, change authorization, release management, and review by a change board.

Relationship of Key Processes

Incident management is focused on restoring normal service and identifies resolution actions; problem management is focused on the identification and resolution of underlying problems and their root causes; and change management deploys changes developed by incident or problem management.

Directory-Services Management

The service directory is a database of service assets. Directory services is essentially a database from which users can obtain information on service assets through a secure and organized process that is accessible through appropriate information and communications technology (ICT) facilities. The major directory service functions are to record change events, describe connectivity, track service objects, and identify assets in the service landscape.

GOVERNANCE

A typical organization has a group of stakeholders who have something to gain if the organization is successful and something to lose if the organization is not successful. The gain could be financial in nature, as in the case of investors, or qualitative in nature, as in the case of non-profit or social organizations. Success or failure is a relative assessment, as is the concept of gain or loss on the part of the stakeholders. The stakeholders, often referred to as the *principles*, give the right to manage the organization to *agents*, ostensibly qualified to do so, and who are rewarded accordingly, through the application of policies and rules that represent the principle's best interests. The process is generally known as governance, a word derived from the Latin verb "to steer." Agents are often high-level or middle-level managers and administrators that derive short and long-term monetary gains that are directly related to the organization's success. There are as many forms of governance as there are organizations to control. Even though the words are similar, governance does not imply local, regional, or central government.

The principles of effective corporate governance are well-defined and usually implemented through "boards of directors" and other governing bodies. Governance is usually related to consistent management, cohesive policies, and effective decision rights. Information technology (IT) governance is generally regarded as a subset of corporate governance, as it relates to the operational management of IT systems. IT governance deals primarily with the connection between business focus and IT management and often involves the organization's IT application portfolio. IT governance is an important consideration in corporate governance because of the typically large budgets for IT infrastructure. *Service governance* is a subset of IT governance that assures the principals that the development and use of services are executed according to best practices.

Two important factors relate to service governance. The first factor involves the high-level of outsourcing of IT functionality and infrastructure. The main concern is the loss of control to an external service provider, and also the long-term loss of capability in critical areas of competence. The second factor is in the evolution to service-oriented architecture for the development of business/enterprise applications. The synthesis of applications from components accessed over the Internet from external service providers constitutes a long-term dependency with which many principals are not comfortable. In this case, the principals may want to use service governance as a means of protecting the long-term interest and possibly the intellectual capital of the parent organization.

QUICK SUMMARY

The main objective of this paper is to present an overview of the dynamically changing boundary of the modern enterprise, based on a portfolio of services. The overview is summarized in the following entries.

1. There are three forces operating in the sphere of service processes. The first is the use of ICT as an enabler in providing revenue growth, efficiency, and effectiveness for traditional and enhanced services, as well as for conventional business processes. This subject is commonly referred to as information systems. The second is the

consulting services domain that provides IT services to external organizations. The third is the use of ICT to manage information systems and services, which is a field of endeavor known as IT Services Management. Briefly said, it is the use of computers to manage the enterprise and also to manage itself.

2. The notion of service has its origin in ancient times and was understood to mean "one person doing something for another." With the advent of civilization and industrialization, the definition of service was implicitly extended to encompass "one person doing something for an organization," usually in the form of employment. At this stage, specialization and entrepreneurship kicked in with all of their rights and privileges, resulting in what we now recognize as the service organization.

3. Information is a critical asset in the operation of an enterprise and in the everyday lives of individuals. In a figurative sense, information is the grease that allows the components to work together. IT is employed to handle the information needed to manage the operations of an enterprise and to aid in making effective decisions. Thus, IT is a service to the enterprise, regardless if that enterprise is concerned with production processes, service operations, government reporting, professional services, scientific services, technical services, or personal services.

4. There are several aspects of IT services that can vary between organizations. Examples are commonplace: computer operations, network management, hardware and software acquisition, system analysis and design, software design, software development, information systems integration, and call center and help desk operation and management. This is a representative set of tasks necessary for sustaining an IT services organization. You can do them yourself; you can have another business entity help you do them; or you can have a business entity do them for you. In the latter two cases, the business process is known as *IT service outsourcing*.

5. The service lifecycle consists of five important elements, listed as follows: Service Strategy, Service Design, Service Transition, Service Operation, and Continuous Improvement.

6. Service quality is a complex arrangement of client expectations, client education, business value, and business utility. It is elusive because clients usually cannot assess quality until after a service event has

been completed. Service providers present quality as adherence to standard operating procedures. Service clients view service quality based on expectations and value creation.

7. Every year, businesses spend millions of dollars on their IT infrastructure consisting of hardware, system software, applications, networks, people, and other organizational assets. With "on demand" computing, they can plug into the wall, figuratively speaking, and only pay for the IT services they use. The concept is called *utility computing* that is accessed as most public utilities. We are going to name the utility computing concept as *e-Services*.

8. A *business model* is a representation of a business emphasizing its purpose, strategies, organization and operational practices, and capabilities. It typically covers the following: core capabilities, partner network, value proposition, customer base, distribution methods, cost structure, and revenue base.

9. A *strategy* has been defined as "A long term plan of action designed to achieve a particular goal," and *governance* as "The set of processes, customs, policies, laws, and institutions affecting the way an endeavor is directed, administered, or controlled."

10. A *strategic asset* is a resource that provides the basis for core competencies, economic benefit, and competitive advantage, thereby enabling a service business to provide distinctive service in the marketplace. Because services are labor intensive, investments in people, processes, knowledge, and infrastructure are directly analogous to investments in resources for production and distribution in capital intensive businesses.

11. The objective of service provisioning – regardless of whether the service involves people processing, possession processing, or information processing – is to provide value to customers through an intrinsic knowledge of customer needs obtained by preparation, analysis, usage patterns, and the application of best practices. Within this perspective, a *service* may be alternately defined as a means of delivering value to customers by facilitating outcomes customers want to achieve without the ownership of specific costs and risks.

12. The objective of a service business is to assist in making resources available to the client as services, and in the process, creating value for both provider and client. The value of a service is determined by a client's expectation of service and the client's perception of the service

that is experienced. Expectations are developed by word of mouth, personal needs, and past experience. The service that is delivered is a complex combination of five attributes: reliability, responsiveness, assurance, empathy, and tangibles.

REFERENCES

[1] Carter, S., The *New Language of Business*, Upper Saddle River, NJ: IBM Press, 2007.

[2] Cherbakov, L., et al., "Impact of service orientation at the business level", *IBM Systems Journal*, Vol. 44, No. 4, 2005.

[3] Clark, J., *Everything you ever wanted to know about ITIL® in less than one thousand words! Connect Sphere Limited, www.connectsphere.com, 2007.*

[4] Collier, D. and J. Evans, *Operations Management: Goods, Services, and Value Chains*, Mason OH: Thomson Higher Education, 2007.

[5] Fitzsimmons, J.A. and M.J. Fitzsimmons, *Service Management: Operations, Strategy, Information Technology* (6th Edition), New York: McGraw-Hill/Irwin, 2008.

[6] Ganek, A. and K. Kloeckner, "An overview of IBM Service Management," *IBM Systems Journal*, Vol. 46, No. 3, 2007.

[7] Hagel, J. and J.S. Brown, *From Push to Pull: Emerging Models for Mobilizing Resources*, www.edgeperspectives.com, 2007.

[8] Heizer, J. and B. Render, *Operations Management* (8th Edition), Upper Saddle River, NJ: Pearson Prentice-Hall, 2006.

[9] Hurwitz, J., Bloor, R., Baroudi, C., and M. Kaufman, *Service Oriented Architecture for Dummies*, Hoboken, NJ: Wiley Publishing, Inc., 2007.

[10] ITIL, *Service Strategy*, London: The Stationary Office, 2007.

[11] itSMF, *An Introductory Overview of ITIL® V3*, itSMF Ltd,, 2007.

[12] Katzan, H., *A View of Services Science*, Southeast Decision Science Institute, Savannah, GA, February 21-23, 2007.

[13] Katzan, H., "Foundations of Service Science: Management and Business" *Journal of Service Science, 1*(2): 1-16, 2008.

[14] Katzan, H., *Service Science: Concepts, Technology, Management,* New York: iUniverse, Inc., 2008.

[15] Krafzig, D., Banke, K., and D. Slama, *Enterprise SOA: Service-Oriented Architecture Best Practices,* Upper Saddle River, NJ: Prentice Hall, 2005.

[16] Metters, R., King-Metters, K., Pullman, M., and S Walton, *Successful Service Operations Management* (2e), Boston: Thomson Course Technology, 2006.

[17] *Microsoft Operations Framework (MOF),* TechNet publication, Microsoft Corporation, www.microsoft.com/MOF, 2008.

[18] Nichols, M., "Quality Tools in a Service Environment,"www.ASQ.org, 2007.

[19] Rappa, M.A., "The utility business model and the future of computing services," *IBM Systems Journal,* Vol. 43, No. 1, 2004.

[20] Wikipedia, *Business Models,* www.wikipedia.com, 2008.

[21] Wikipedia, *Corporate Governance,* www.wikipedia.com, 2008.

[22] Wikipedia, *Governance,* www.wikipedia.com, 2008.

[23] Wikipedia, *Information Technology Governance,* www.wikipedia.com, 2008.

[24] Wikipedia, *Software as a Service,* www.wikipedia.com, 2008.

[25] Wikipedia, *Strategy,* www.wikipedia.com, 2008.

[26] Wikipedia, *Thinking Processes,* www.wikipedia.com, 2008.

[27] Woods, D. and T. Mattern, *Enterprise SOA: Designing IT for Business Innovation,* Sebastopol, CA: O'Reilly Media Inc., 2006.

***** End of Essay 4 *****

5

SERVICE TECHNOLOGY AND ARCHITECTURE

SERVICE TECHNOLOGY CONCEPTS

The basis of service technology is really straightforward. Clients and providers communicate with one another through the use of messages and contracts, and in many areas of service, the communication involves information and communications technology (ICT). A client and a provider can be tightly coupled, as when a patient is sitting in front of the doctor and they are having a give-and-take conversation, or loosely coupled, as when you send a request to someone via email and receive a response at some undetermined time in the future. In the former case, the client and provider are communicating in a *synchronous mode* without technology, and in the latter case, they are communicating in an *asynchronous mode* with the use of technology. The *contract* is a formal or informal agreement that delineates the service in which the client and provider are engaged. The contract can be a formal document, an informal agreement, or be implicit in the activity under consideration. Another view of a contract is that it is a specification of how to use a service and what to expect from a service.

Messaging Basics

Each service event requires at least one message, and each message requires a context, which gives meaning to the interaction. Entities that participate in a service-oriented message are called the message sender, the message intermediary, and the message receiver. When you fire up your Internet browser, for example, and enter a World Wide Web address, such as www.ibm.com, the browser sends a message to the IBM server somewhere out in cyberspace. The browser, acting on your behalf, as the client of the Web service, is the message sender. The IBM web site is the message receiver. When IBM sends its home page back to be rendered for you by your browser, the roles are reversed; it is the sender and your browser is the receiver, and the Internet is the message intermediary. The *message* is the glue that ties a service together.

Conceptual Model of Service Processing

The most profound aspect of service science is that a *service is a process*, as suggested by the following message pattern:

1. A client sends a message to a service provider.
2. The provider performs the required action and returns a message to the client.

The focus is on the data that is transmitted and not on the communications medium, which can take the form of a human interaction or a computer-based message. The context for the message can be embedded in the message or it can be inherent in the way that the service provider is addressed. The importance of context is suggested by the cartoon floating around where two dogs are seated in front of a computer screen. One dog says to the other, "On the Internet, no one knows you're a dog." Two good rules of thumb are that in face-to-face services, interpersonal communication provides the context. In human-to-computer services, the context must be inherent in the message. For example, entering "Boston Red Sox" into your browser to get the score of the last World Series game is probably going to generate a lot of miscellaneous information in which you are not interested, because you provided no context.

Initially, it is useful to recognize that we are operating at two levels: the service level and the message level. At the *service level*, the message entity that receives the message is the service provider and is regarded simply as the **service**. At the *message level*, there is some choreography involved with providing a service, as demonstrated by the above two-step interaction. In fact, a service may involve the interchange of several messages.

Enterprise Service Technology

Many modern enterprises (i.e., business, government, education) provide computer support to internal users, clients, business partners, and other enterprise entities. The facilities are usually integrated into administrative, product development, supply chain, or customer relationship operations. Because those services, consisting of computer applications and associated procedures, are tried, tested, and dependable, it would be prudent to use them as building blocks for new enterprise applications.

The concept that underlies service orientation is that it is simply more efficient and reliable in identifying the bundled services and packaging them as reusable components than it would be to rewrite them. Bundled services could then be used by other services, so that information system applications could be developed more rapidly and enable the enterprise to be more responsive to external conditions. This practice is the basis of web services that are covered in this paper.

A typical business function that lends itself to componentization is to perform a credit check on a prospective customer before confirming a large order. Such a check is normally performed in different operational systems in an enterprise. After restructuring, the credit check software is packaged as a single business component and exposed as an enterprise service for use by other enterprise service applications.

SERVICE MESSAGING

When two service entities are engaged in communication, they are regarded as being *connected*. An enterprise has two options for developing a service connection:

1. Message entity to message entity (ME→ME)
2. Message entity to enterprise entity (ME→EE)

The first option, denoted by ME → ME, refers to either a client-to-provider or a provider-to-client communication. The second option denoted by ME → EE refers to a client-to-many-provider communication. The notion of connectedness is needed for an appreciation of message patterns and topologies, covered in the next section. For example, the ME→ME option may represent the case where an order-processing application sends a message to a shipping application to have an item shipped to a customer. The ME➔EE option might represent the case where an airline's flight operations application sends a message to other involved computer applications, such as scheduling and reservations, when a plane has taken off.

Message Patterns

A *message pattern* is a model of service communications that represents a single connection between one sender and one receiver. There are three basic patterns representing message traffic that can go only one way, both ways but only one way at a time, and both ways simultaneously.

The one-way message flow is regarded as a "fire-and-forget-it" send, also known as *simplex* and *datagram* communications service in the computer community. The second model is the request/reply model, known as *half duplex*, wherein only one participant communicates at a time as with the walkie-talkie type of interaction. In the final model, called *full duplex*, both messaging participants can send messages at the same time, as in an ordinary telephone conversation. Clearly, messaging can take on different patterns depending upon the operational environment used for technical support.

Message Structure

In its simplist form, a message is a string of characters encoded using standardized coding methods commonly employed in computer and information technology. Messages have a uniform format consisting of a header and a body. The *header* primarily concerns addressing and includes the addresses of the sender and the receiver. In the request/reply message pattern, the return address is picked up from the message header for the response portion of the transaction. The *body* of the message contains the information content of the message, and because it is intended only for the receiver, is not usually regarded during message transmission.

The manner in which messages are structured is similar to the way that letters are handled by the postal service. The outside of the envelope contains addressing information and the insides are handled as private information.

Message Topology

Message topology refers to the manner in which messages are sent between messaging participants, and not necessarily to the communication techniques used to send them. The most widely used form of communication is known as *point-to-point* using any of the message patterns given above. Usually, point-to-point implies the request/reply message pattern where the reply address is picked up from the message header. A variation to point-to-point is *forward-only point-to-point* where a message reply is not expected.

Message Interactions

In most cases of messaging, the sending participant needs to know that the receiving participant is listening before the real message is transmitted. It is something like the following:

Sender: Are you listening?
Receiver: Yes.
Sender: Are you Gregory Charles Cabot?
Receiver: Yes.
Sender: You've just won one million dollars.

OK, it's a bit contrived and also, it's messaging at the service level. There is also handshaking going on at the message level, which we are going to cover in the next section.

The following example demonstrates message interaction through instant messaging at the service level. It demonstrates message interactions. (This example is adapted from Van Slyke and Bélanger, p. 110.) For this instance, **User A** is sending an instant message to **User B** who responds to **User A.** The interaction consists of four distinct messages, delineated as follows:

> Message 1: User A logs on to the instant messaging (IM) server. The expected response is that the IM server will return a message from the users in A's group that are currently logged on. The message goes from User A through the Internet to the IM server.

Message 2: The IM server sends a message to User A with the members that are logged on. The message goes from the IM server to User A.

Message 3 : User A sends a message, such as "Hi User B," to User B. The message goes from User A through the Internet to the IM server. The IM server then sends the message through the Internet to User B.

Message 4: User B responds with a message, such as "Hi yourself," to User A. The message goes through the Internet to the IM server. Then the IM server sends the message through the Internet to User A.

Most people would regard this interaction sequence in which User A sends an instant message to User B as a service and B's response to A as another service. Popping up a level, the service provider is the instant messaging server and users A and B are clients.

SERVICES ON THE INTERNET AND THE WORLD WIDE WEB

A service that takes place on the Internet and the World Wide Web is called a *web service*. A web service is a process in which the provider and client interact to produce a value; it is a pure service. The only difference between a web service and medical provisioning, for example, is that in the former case, the client and provider are computer systems. Ordinary email is a web service. Requesting a home page from a provider's web site is a web service. Sending an instant message over the Internet is a web service. Almost anything you can think of doing on the web would be called a web service. However, there is another category of service known as a Web Service. Note that Web Service is a proper noun. It is a formal process, developed by organizations such as Microsoft, Apple, and others, for conducting business over the Internet. It is covered separately.

Simple Mail Model

The most pervasive web service computer application on the Internet is electronic mail, commonly known as email. It is used in two ways: (1) To communicate between email clients; and (2) To provide a record that communication has taken place – or at least, to show that an attempt at communication has taken place. Clearly, email is designed to be a person-to-person endeavor. There are two scenarios that are relevant to web services.

In the first scenario, we have a desktop personal computer (PC) operating as an email client – referred to as a PC running an email client – from which the end user sends and receives email. The email client is connected to incoming and outgoing email servers through a local-area network or a dial-up, broadband cable, or DSL connection to an Internet service provider (ISP) that is in turn connected to the mail servers. Email messages are normally managed locally, which means they are downloaded and stored on the end user's computer. When the end user decides to access email messages, he or she presses a receive button and incoming messages, stored on the incoming email server, are transferred to the local email client. Similarly, when the end user constructs a message for sending, a send key is pressed to transfer it to the outgoing email server for subsequent forwarding over the Internet. An email client uses push technology to send email messages and pull technology to receive email messages.

In the second scenario, we again have an email client for message management. The email client, however, is connected to an email-service server via the Internet through a local browser. The service access point is an account set up on an Internet service portal. A web based email account is used in the same manner as in the local scenario, except that the email server is remote.

The concept of a remote service server is also a platform for other web applications, such as word processing and spreadsheet operations. A remote service server that provides application functionality is known as an *application service provider*, and exists as an alternative to purchasing infrequently used software.

Service Model for the World Wide Web

When addressing a web service, there is a certain way that most people go about doing things. It's not entirely clear whether the web service architecture determines how people use the web or, the other way around, whether the architecture of the web reflects how people use it. We are calling it a generic web services model.

Imagine the following scenario. You're interested in purchasing a pair of running shoes and don't know any brands or web sites. So what do you do? You point your browser to a search engine, such as Google™, enter the words "running shoes" in the search window and click the "search" button or press the enter key. Your message is sent to Google's web server that searches an index of key words, created beforehand, and makes a list of appropriate web sites, just for you. The web server then prepares your list in a language called HTML and sends it back to your browser over the Internet. The browser then renders the HTML statements into a readable form. This is an example of the first element in the web services model. It's known as *discovery*. The service process was accomplished without regard to time, distance, or the kind of hardware and software.

Each of the entries (known as a "hit") on the resultant running-shoe list gives a brief description and a *hyperlink* with which to obtain more definitive information. This process reflects the second element in the web services model, and it is known as *description*. Various enterprises have web sites and associated web pages containing descriptive information of interest. In a separate operation, the organization behind the search engine searches the web sites in cyberspace and prepares indexes for fast retrieval.

If your goal is information, then this is perhaps as far as you will go with this example. If you are going to make a purchase over the web using an appropriate site, then the next step is to *bind* to that web site and go through an interactive process for selection, payment, and delivery. Each step in the bind process requires additional web services, so that a web service is essentially a cascading series of other web services.

A variety of tools and techniques are required for a successful implementation of web services architecture. Whenever there is a service, there is communication; and whenever there is communication, there are messages. Whenever there is a message, there is a context so that the intent of the service can be sustained. These elements are present in one form or another in all services, ranging from the more straightforward human interaction to the operation of a sophisticated enterprise computer application.

HyperText Transfer Protocol

HyperText Transfer Protocol (HTTP) is a collection of rules and procedures for transferring messages between computers over the World Wide Web. Without HTTP, the web would not be the revolutionary phenomena that it is today. When you make a service request over the web, your entry goes through your browser before it goes over the Internet. Here's how.

When you fire up your browser, you are initiating the execution of a program that runs on your personal computer, workstation, personal digital assistant (PDA), cell phone, terminal – or whatever you choose to use. Now that computing device is performing a service for you in the sense that you can now do things you could not possibly do without it. In fact, you could run all manner of programs, such as productivity software that does word processing, without any information leaving or entering your local environment. As far as the Internet is concerned, however, essentially nothing has happened. You type a URL into your browser window and press the enter key, and then things start to happen. This is when HTTP gets into the act.

Your browser prepares a message called a HTTP request, such as

GET /index.html HTTP/1.1
Host: www.example.com

and sends it over the Internet to the web server of the "example.com" web site somewhere out in cyberspace. The web server responds in turn to the return address obtained from your message header with

HTTP/1.1 200 OK
Date: Mon, 02 Dec 2007 12:38:34 GMT
Server: Apache/1.3.27 (Unix) (Red-Hat/Linux)
Last-Modified: Wed, 08 Jan 2003 23:11:55 GMT
Etag: "3f80f-1b6-3e1cb03b"
Accept-Ranges: bytes
Content-Length: 155
Connection: close
Content-Type: text/html; charset=UTF-8

This response message is followed by a blank line and then the requested information that represents the contents of the file (usually the default file, such as index.html) from the site specified in the HTTP get request. The information content of the response message might take the form (highly unlikely but possible):

```
<html>
    <head>
        <title>Hello World</title>
    </head>
    <body>
        <h1>Hello World</h1>
        <par>
        Greetings from Cyberspace
        </par>
    </body>
</html>
```

that would be rendered by your browser and displayed on your screen. The text is transmitted in a well-known language peculiar to the web and known as HyperText Markup Language (HTML). It is introduced in the next section.

The *HyperText Transfer Protocol* has additional verbs, such as POST, PUT, and DELETE, that facilitate the transfer of messages between a client computer and a server computer.

HYPERTEXT MARKUP LANGUAGE

Aside from the Internet information super highway and the idea of linking information pages together (i.e., the World Wide Web), probably the coolest thing that has ever happened in the over-hyped world of computers, is the realization that it is possible to send a document from one computer to another and have that document displayed on the receiving end in a reasonable form without regard to the brand and model of computer, kind of software, time of day, and location. This amazing feat – and it is truly that – is possible because of hypertext markup language (HTML), as introduced in the previous section. We are interested in HTML for two important reasons. First, it is a useful thing to know something about, as long as you don't get hung up in the details. Secondly, HTML is a forerunner to Extensible Markup Language (XML) that is a technology for sending messages between services.

HTML Documents

To start off, an HTML document is nothing more than a bunch of characters that someone has entered into a text editor or a word processor and saved as a file on a computer employed as a web server. When you request an answer from a web site, such as the one and only www.ibm.com, the corresponding web server goes to a default file named index.html, retrieves the HTML file, and sends it back to your browser for rendering on your computer's display. It is someone's job to put the right stuff into index.html, and that stuff should be written in HTML. Now the file named index.html might have links to other pages that are returned in a similar manner when you click on them. Those links are referred to as *hot links*, because we get some action when we click on them – as we just mentioned. You can even put programs into an HTML document. These programs are executed by your browser resulting in some visual or audio activity on the receiving end. The active behavior can result in a wide variety of audio, video, and data-oriented interactive forms.

Tags

The basis of an HTML is a tag, such as <html>, that provides information to the receiving browser. In the case of <html>, for example, the tag indicates the beginning of an HTML document. Actually, a tag is only a strong suggestion, since each browser has a mind of its own. Most tags have an enclosing tag, such as </html>, that delineates a section of a document, such as in the following HTML snippet:

```
<html>
    <head>
        <title>University of the United States</title>
    </head>
    <body>
    •
    •    ←--- The content goes here
    •
    </body>
</html>
```

Tags give an HTML document structure and information on page rendering; they do not give meaning. We will use XML for that.

Discovery

One of the key aspects of web page design is to facilitate discovery, whereby clients can find services. Search engine companies use a technique known as "web crawling" in which a program called a *web crawler* or a *bot* (for robot) crawls through web pages following hyperlinks to build indexes for subsequent search operations. Without additional information, all words in a web page are treated the same. You can add additional information to the "head" section to increase the fidelity of searching and increase the chances that a user will navigate to your web site.

This is where the <meta> tag comes in. With the meta tag, web page designers commonly supply three types of descriptive items: a list of keywords, a description, and the name of the web page owner – sometimes the name of an organization and sometimes an author. Search bots use this information when building indexes. The following example depicts the use of meta tags:

```
<html>
    <head>
        <title>Savannah Motor Works</title>
        <meta name="keywords" content="Porsche, Mercedes, BMW">
        <meta name="description" content="The south's most prestigious performance car dealership">
        <meta name="author" content="Gregory Cabot">
    </head>
    <body>
    •
    •
    •
    </body>
</html>
```

Actually, there are no predefined meta tags in HTML, so a web page designer can create them to satisfy a particular need. The meta tag demonstrates a tag without an enclosing tag.

Document Elements

The HTML language has an extensive vocabulary that is a subject in its own right. A brief subset of HTML features is covered here as a forerunner to Extensible Markup Language (XML) that is used to construct messages between clients and service providers. Some of the most commonly used document elements are <h1> through <h6>, <p>, <b>, <i>, <br>, and <hr>, which represent headings, paragraph, bold face, italics, blank line, and horizontal rule, respectively. Several of these elements are depicted in the following script:

```
<html>
    <head>
        <title>My First Novel</title>
    </head>
    <body bgcolor="yellow">
        <h1 align="center">The Car</h1>
        <p align="center"> <i>by</i> </p>
        <p align="center"> <b>Gregory Cabot</b></p>
        <p> My uncle gave me my first car. It was a 1939 Chevy with
        fluid drive. It had a flat tire and the brakes didn't work. It also
        had a broken window.
        </p>
        <p> My father taught me how to do the repairs and I had to
        do them.
        Afterwards, I didn't like the car and sold it for $50.
        </p>
        <hr>
        <p align="center">The End</p>
    </body>
</html>
```

Of course, complete comprehension is not necessary or even expected. However, the key point has been made that HTML is a powerful tool in the construction and communication of web-based documents.

EXTENSIBLE MARKUP LANGUAGE

To put the virtues of HTML and XML into perspective, we can properly say that HTML is used to describe web pages and XML is used to describe information. XML stands for eXtensible Markup Language. Both languages use markup, a term that ostensibly is intended to imply that someone prepares a document and then incorporates descriptive elements to suggest how the document should look when displayed *or* to communicate the intended meaning of the document. With XML, markup gives semantic information as suggested by the following script:

```
<?xml version="1.0" ?>
<library>
     <library_name>Pleasure Books</ library_name>
     <book>
          <title>The DaVinci Code</title>
          <author>Dan Brown</author>
     </book>
     <book>
          <title>The Secret Servant</title>
          <author>Daniel Silva</author>
     </book>
</library>
```

We will call the semantic information "tags" as we did with HTML, even though XML specialists refer to them as "element type names." An XML document must contain a

prolog and at least one enclosing document element. In the above example, the following statement is the prolog:
<?xml version="1.0" ?>and the enclosing document element is:
    <library>
      ●

- ●
- ●

```
</library>
```

This is an example of a main element that must be present in all XML documents. It is often referred to as the *root element*, and it is the characteristic that gives an XML document a hierarchical structure. All opening tags in XML, such as <book>, must have closing tags, such as </book>. With XML, we can make up our own tags, since we are using the language to describe information that has a specific meaning.

Rendering an XML Document

Even though an XML document, by definition, is intended for communication, we can display the contents in a particular form by using a stylesheet. To use a stylesheet, we have to extend the prolog with a statement of the form:

```
<?xml:stylesheet href="library.css" type="text/css" ?>
```

and develop a stylesheet description file, named library.css in this example, that would have descriptive content, such as the following:

```
library_name {
      display: block;
      font: bold 24pt;
}
title {
      margin-top: 20px;
      display: block;
      font: italic 18pt;
}
author {
      display: block;
      font: 12pt;
}
```

A rendering of the penultimate XML document would be achieved with the library.css stylesheet file.

Additional XML Features

There is a lot more to the XML language, such as a formal means of defining data types and stylistic structures for XML documents along with a whole host of operational facilities. If it would take one book to totally describe HTML, it would take two books to fully give the features in XML. For a basic knowledge of service science, complete comprehension of XML is not needed – only an idea of what it is all about.

At this point, we have enough knowledge of service tools and techniques to proceed with Web Services, introduced in the next section. We are going to start with a specification of the XML grammar for a form of web messaging known as SOAP, which was initially an acronym for Simple Object Access Protocol.

WEB SERVICES

A Web Service has been defined as any service that is available over the Internet, uses a standard XML messaging system, and is not dependant upon any one particular operating system. (See E. Cerami, *Web Services Essentials* (Selected Reading), for much of the subject matter in this section.) This statement has the makings of something different from the "web service" that was presented earlier when discussing HTTP. Well, it is. Earlier, we described the human web wherein an end-user sends an informational request via HTTP to a web server, and the requested information is returned, also via HTTP, to the user's browser for visual display. In this section, we are going to cover the automated web, in which one computer sends information, in the form of an XML document, to another computer over the Internet, and the intended result is to initiate a service of some kind. The latter form is a well-defined web service model such that the name Web Service is a proper noun. It is important to mention that XML is used for things other than Web Services. In just so happens that they grew up together, so that they are naturally associated with one another.

Web Service Concepts

There are two general approaches to using a Web Service. The first is to have one computer (*the sender*) send a simple message to a second computer (*the receiver*) to have the receiver execute a procedure for the sender and return the result. The procedure is known as a *method* and the process is referred to as an XML-RPC, which stands for *XML-Remote Procedure Call*. A frequently used example to demonstrate the concept is the weather service application: a requester sends a zip code to the weather service program and the program (i.e., the method) returns the temperature. The initial request message can be written in XML as:

```
<?xml version="1.0"?>
<weatherRPC>
      <weatherMethod>getTemperature</weatherMethod>
      <parameters>
            <zip_code>29909</zip_code>
      </ parameters >
</weatherRPC>
```

The example is conceptual and the message headers and other information are omitted. The response from the weather service would take the form:

```
<?xml version="1.0"?>
      <weatherResponse>
      <parameters>
            <value><int>75</int></value>
      </parameters>
</weatherResponse>
```

XML-RPC can be implemented via an HTTP request/response or by embedding the informational content of the transaction in a SOAP message, which is the second approach.

SOAP is a protocol for exchanging information between computers where the structure of the information is represented in XML. The basic idea underlying SOAP messaging is to make sure that programs running on two communicating computer platforms have the capability of understanding each other. Accordingly, the XML element definitions from several namespaces need to be specified in a standard manner and also be accessible over the Internet. We are not going to include the definitions, per se, in the SOAP message, but instead, include a reference to the definitions, so that if things change, every message in the world does not have to change.

A simplex (i.e., one-way) message from a client to a server or from a server to a client is called a *SOAP message* and consists of a SOAP envelope in which is placed a message header and a message body. The optional header is intended to allow the inclusion of application-specific information, such as security and account numbers. The required message body contains the references and informational content of the SOAP message. Here is what the SOAP envelope looks like:

```
<SOAP-ENV:Envelope
    xmlns:SOAP-ENV="http://schemas.xmlsoap.org/soap/envelope/"
    xmlns:xsi="http://www.w3.org/2001/XMLSchema-instance"
    xmlns:xsd="http://www.w3.org/2001/XMLSchema">
    •
    •    ←----- The message body would go here
    •
</SOAP-ENV:Envelope>
```

and a sample message body is

```
<SOAP-ENV:Body>
    <ns1:getTemp
    xmlns:ns1="urn:xmethods-Temperature"
    SOAP-ENV:encodingStyle="http://schemas.xmlsoap.org/soap/
     encoding/">
        <zipcode xsi:type="xsd:string">29909</zipcode>
    </ns1:getTemp>
</SOAP-ENV:Body>
```

Again, comprehension is not required or expected. The scripts are exceedingly detailed, but one point is clear, even from this simple example. Once the structure of SOAP messaging is developed, the addition of the content can be quite straightforward.

To sum up this section, SOAP messaging is straightforward. All one SOAP client has to do to send a message to another SOAP client is to put the content document into a predetermined SOAP message structure and send it through the Internet. It doesn't matter if the sender is a client or a server, as long as the sender and the receiver are both SOAP clients. The message itself is not important to the messaging process. It could be a request to have a method executed, or it could be a document, such as a financial report or a script representing a computer graphics procedure.

Web Service Model

In order to request a service over the Internet, a person must go through a standard procedure. We covered this earlier. There are three roles: the service provider, the service requester, and the service registry. The *service provider* makes a service available over the Internet. The *service requester* consumes a service by sending an XML message to the service provider over the Internet. The *service registry* is a centralized repository of information about services that are available, serving as a computer-oriented version of the traditional "yellow pages."

Associated with the three roles are three activities. The service provider publishes available services in the service registry. The service requester finds out about services by accessing the service registry. The service requester invokes a service (called *bind*) by sending an XML message, referred to above, to the service provider. A familiar example of publish, find, and bind is an online book service. The prospective buyer consults the company's online catalog to find a suitable book. The buyer then finalizes the purchasing process by providing the requisite information, and the seller handles the billing and the physical transportation of the item purchased.

There is more to it, of course. When a service provider publishes service information, it must be described in a form that the service requester can understand. XML is used for this task by employing a document structure known a UDDI, which stands for *Universal Description, Discovery, and Integration*. When a service requester invokes a service, XML is again used in a form of descriptive language known as WSDL, which stands for *Web Services Description Language*.

Web Service Goal

The goal of Web Services was, and still, is the process of having computers talk to each other to arrange for a service without human intervention. At this stage, the Internet community has done a commendable job of establishing the requisite technical infrastructure, but the process still requires client interaction at the service-requester end. The focus is currently on building a service-oriented architecture to support future developments.

SERVICE ARCHITECTURE CONCEPTS

Service architecture is a collection of design patterns for constructing services from building blocks that can be shared between service systems. Most business processes already incorporate a form of service architecture, since the principles are derived from ordinary common sense. For example, many accounting departments include component services, such as credit checking and invoicing. When the objective is to align information services with business processes, however, the design gets more complicated and has given rise to a field of study known as *service-oriented architecture* (SOA). The basic idea behind service architecture is that you have a collection of components, representing business functions or computer applications, and you want to fit them together to make a business process or an information system. Components encapsulate services so that a service-oriented application or a business process is assimilated from multiple components that achieve the desired functionality by collectively orchestrating the operation of the needed services. The guiding principle behind service-oriented architecture is that once a component is established, it can be reused in other applications or business processes. Eventually, an organization runs out of components to build so that the synthesis of an application or a business process becomes a matter of piecing the components together – much like the manner in which an aircraft manufacturer or automobile company assembles relatively complicated products from off-the-shelf or specially-designed components. There are two aspects to the idea of building functionality with components; the first is putting the components together, and the second is making the inherent services interact in such a way that a desired state of business process engineering (BPE) is achieved.

Solution Life Cycle

An effective solution sequence for any development project incorporates a set of well-defined steps, such as the following: requirements analysis, modeling, architectural design, detailed design, construction, and testing. In the modern view of development, incorporating service architecture principles, these steps are divided into two phases: the *preproduction phase*, wherein a set of packaged components are collected, and the *production phase*, consisting of assembly and deployment.

It is important to recognize that the term "production" in the context of service life cycle refers to the synthesis of a business process or the development of an information system, and not to the actual utilization of the process or system, as in everyday operations. So, in a sense, we are producing a solution and not using a solution. Once we have the wherewithal to assemble a solution from components and do not have to develop those components from scratch, then we can spend our resources making sure that the eventual solution to whatever problem we are dealing with actually satisfies business needs – and is developed in a reasonable time frame. This is where the term *agility* comes from. The management of an enterprise, for example, perceives that it needs an IT solution to an e-commerce opportunity, and the IT department can expeditiously deliver that solution.

On Demand

The term "on demand" seems to have navigated its way into the business literature in at least three ways. In the first instance, on demand refers to the access of information, such as from the World Wide Web or any other information repository, from wherever the end user may be and whenever the interaction takes place. In the second instance, on demand refers to access to computer application programs without specifically having to purchase them. Also known as *utility computing*, this form of on demand would allow end user to pay only for the use of software, rather than having to purchase it, as is typically the case with traditional office software. Finally, the third instance of on demand and the one in which we are interested refers to the techniques for the rapid development of business processes and computer information systems to support enterprise services.

The flexibility inherent in on demand services provides a payback for most enterprises that is greater than the value of the processes and applications for which the services were originally intended. Overall, on demand processes developed through service orientation can deliver innovation, flexibility, shorter time to market, and they also serve as a vehicle for rethinking industry structures. (Cherbakov, et al., 2005) In fact, the business value of service architecture is perhaps best summarized by the following quotation from the same paper by Cherbakov, Galambos, Harishankar, Kalyana, and Rackham: (op cit. p. 654):

> What is described here is a business that is able to recognize change as it is occurring and react appropriately, ahead of the competition, and keep pace with demands of its customers, value-net partners, and employees alike. In trying to achieve this state, the business will need to leverage technology to the fullest. We call such a business an "on demand business." Fundamentally, becoming an on demand business is equivalent to achieving total business flexibility. Two important enablers contribute to the realization by an enterprise of this vision of on demand – componentization and service orientation.

Components are related to functions – or to be more specific, business components are related to business functions. In a real sense, therefore, service architecture refers to the deconstruction into components of an existing business system, and subsequently, its reconstruction into an operational network of cooperating and integrated elements needed for synthesizing responsive enterprise-wide systems.

Components, Services, and Functions

It's all relatively straightforward: most components encapsulate one or more services; many complex services require more than one component; enterprise processes are constructed from components; and enterprise functions are an amalgamation of corresponding services. The notion of putting components together to achieve some enterprise function is called *composability*, and in order to do this, the methodology demands severe constraints on the manner in which the components are constructed and packaged for reuse. Components must fit together in order to operate as intended; this requirement is known as *interoperability*.

Service Orientation

Many people are going to say that dealing with a collection of interacting components is just going to increase the complexity of their everyday life. After all, they say, why not buy an application program or adopt an established business process and be done with it? On the other hand, there is something to be said for building systems out of packaged components. If a component fails, replace the entire assembly and let the customer – or should be say client – pay for it. After all, that perspective has some merit with products and is widely adopted. The point to remember is, "What's good for products is not necessarily good for services." Here are some of the reasons.

Because services are heterogeneous and involve client interaction, most service interactions are essentially different, so that the unrestricted use of packaged facilities does not automatically contribute to efficiency. With both products and services, features sell packaged facilities, so that if you obtain two related packages, there would normally be a duplication of functionality. In other words, organizations that produce packages, in the most general sense, include as many features as possible to optimize marketability. Most of us THINK products and DO services. Moreover, there is no guarantee that similar components in different packages operate – or interoperate – in exactly the same manner.

Another consideration is that in the area of professional, scientific, and technical services, the operant process is to construct a flexible system, perhaps for a client, in which components can be replaced on a demand basis to satisfy business conditions. In this instance, one would want each component to be designed as granular as possible with a well-defined interface.

SERVICE DEVELOPMENT

One of the basic tenets of service science is that service providers can participate in a service experience by applying knowledge, skill, ingenuity, and experience, without having to invest in the usual encumbrances of product development. In this section, we are going to cover *service development*, without having to necessarily develop each and every service resource. The subject matter primarily concerns "legacy systems," and the methodology applies to just about any kind of service an ordinary person can imagine.

Legacy Systems

Many, if not most, information systems used in business, education, and government are known as *legacy systems* and continue to be the core of enterprise technology. For example, the "grunt" work underlying heavy duty data processing is performed behind the scenes, often during the wee hours of the night by mainframe computers. Linking these systems to modern Web services has been difficult, because they are difficult to change without running the risk of upsetting the applecart of good performance. The programs are written primarily in the COBOL programming language and precise specifications are not always available, adding another dimension to the problem.

Information systems that are cumbersome to change are referred to as being "brittle" and limit an enterprise's ability to respond to changing business requirements. On the other hand, legacy systems are serious assets to an organization and typically represent considerable investments. In many cases, organizations achieve a level of competitive advantage through the use of legacy systems. Legacy systems support day-to-day operations and incorporate the business logic inherent in all areas of the business model.

Service architecture purports to leverage legacy systems by unlocking the business functionality through loosely-coupled, but well-structured, service components abducted from legacy systems. The service components can then be choreographed to adapt or extend business processes to satisfy current needs. This can be achieved in two ways: leveraging or repurposing. With *leveraging*, the functions in legacy systems are exposed without rewriting the system. With *repurposing*, the programs are rewritten for the modern world with a modern language, such as Java, for use on servers designed for the Internet and the World Wide Web. Clearly, leveraging is the way to go with legacy systems, because of the risk involved with rewriting large programs and getting it right the first time.

Exposing Functionality in Legacy System

Exposing business services by leveraging legacy systems is not a simple matter, and it requires good strategic planning, time, and considerable resources. Typically, the work is outsourced to IT consulting companies, because a high level of expertise is required, but not otherwise needed, to sustain enterprise operations.

Although the task is exceedingly complex, the idea is relatively simple: put a software wrapper around the legacy code and expose what you want to expose through well-defined interfaces. The conceptual software wrapper is known as an *adapter*.

Here's how it works. One component needs the services of another component, which may reside locally or be available over the Internet residing somewhere out in cyberspace. The needy component sends an XML message to the servicing component requesting a service of some kind. What this means is that the serving component does something and returns the result as an XML message to the requestor. The messages adhere to an agreed-upon format so that the programs can understand each other.

The overall process is not much different from when one person asks another person for the time. The requestor issues the request in a socially agreed upon language in a well-defined format. The responder accesses a time resource and returns the time in the same language and in a related but different format. If another person asks for the time, the process is repeated.

There are some hidden components in the messaging scenario. The requestor needs information on who would know the actual time. So an internal registry of "people who know about time" is implicitly consulted before the initial message is sent by the requester to the responder. With service architecture, a registry of components is needed to know which components to call upon when a particular service is needed. Part of the registry process could very well involve a search process to determine which registry contains the needed information. Then, perhaps, the requestor might engage a local registry to store pertinent information from non-local registries to facilitate subsequent operations.

SERVICE REFERENCE ARCHITECTURE

A certain amount of structure among components is required for the capabilities, mentioned above, to function together as a coherent whole. It is commonly known as the *SOA Reference Architecture*. The reference architecture is essentially a stack of functionality, implying that service messages flow upward and downward in the stack.

Loose Coupling

The basic principle of service architecture is that synthesis involves composition. A business process or a computer application is created by combining independent components that are loosely coupled. *Loose coupling*, in this instance, simply means that components – that is, the components providing the services – pass requests and data, in the form of messages, between each other in a standard manner without the need for underlying assumptions that would compromise component operational interdependence. Thus, a small change in the functioning of one component would not require a change to other components that rely on the changed component. With component architecture of this sort, it is important to recognize that components normally relate to enterprise-level processes spanning people, systems, and information.

Services

Services can be created or exposed. In the former case, an organization creates the business process or a computer application from scratch. In the latter case, an existing service is insulated with a logical container and its functionality is explicitly described so that other entities can use it. It's entirely possible that a service developed for another generation doesn't exactly fit in with what you are doing. In this instance, an adapter is needed to make whatever adjustments are necessary to use the service. It's like using your spouse as an adapter to your mother-in-law to arrange for babysitting service. In the world of computers, an *adapter* is a software module that permits access to a service through a standard messaging interface, usually created through the XML language.

Combining diverse services and exposing them as a single service is commonplace in everyday life. Consider, for example, a delivery service that combines three capabilities: dispatcher, driver, and accountant. The dispatcher interacts with the customers and makes the arrangements for the deliveries. The driver organizes his or her delivery route and makes the deliveries. The accountant records transactions, sends bills, and records payments. Yet, to the customer, there is only one service interface, which, in fact, is the point where the package is submitted for transportation. The delivery service has been composed from the three component services and the total process is called *composition*. Facilities, sometimes called *tools*, are needed to put references to components and corresponding services in the registry so that system designers can find them. All of this points to why the subject of web services is so important. Web services with its associated XML, SOAP, UDDI, and WSDL facilities, provide a convenient means of establishing a reference architecture.

Messaging

The messaging layer of the service reference architecture provides the means for the components to interact and emphasizes the need for in-between functionality to provide the requisite level of independence required by SOA Reference Architecture. Consider, for example, an investment firm that supports a database of up-to-the-second stock prices. An investment advisor with a client on the line would like the latest price of AT&T stock. So he or she enters the stock exchange code for AT&T, namely 'T', and presses a key on the advisor's workstation. In a flash, the current stock price is returned. Some in-between hardware and software, known as *middleware*, is required to make it all happen. Clearly, many other services within the investment firm would also utilize the same stock price service. It's a simple example but gives evidence that the component-based approach to system development has some definite merit.

A messaging service would normally use *asynchronous messaging*, which means that the requestor sends the message to the service and the result is returned as soon as possible. While the person may be waiting for a response operating in a synchronous mode, the underlying hardware and software goes along its merry way sending messages back and forth asynchronously. Because of the great difference in processing speeds of humans and computers, it appears as though the computer is sitting there waiting for a request and responds immediately. In reality, that request may be put on a queue and processed in order of arrival, recognizing that different methods for queue management may be used.

Registry

The concept of a registry was introduced previously in the context of legacy systems and web services. With web services, the registry is a general facility for storing service information that can be retrieved through XML messaging. It's more complicated but that's the idea. With service architecture, as in the present context, the registry is a repository for information on components, intended for persons synthesizing a composite service, and additionally contains tools to assist in achieving that synthesis. *The registry is a data base of components and the services they supply.*

The registry should also contain facilities for convenient search, the import and export of entries, and change management. In the latter instance, it is necessary for users to be informed of updates that might affect their performance.

The registry should additionally reflect business policy as it refers to distribution, security, and ownership.

Architecture Services Management

In the present context, services management refers to the operation and management control over business processes constructed with a service orientation. The efficacy of service operations is always of concern as it relates to service-level agreements as they relate to performance and quality of service. In the former case, performance encompasses the availability and reliability of individual services. In the latter case, quality of service refers to the statistical analysis of specific service events.

Management control reflects governance concepts as they apply to the operations mission, previously mentioned. Governance should reflect the fact that service architecture is a methodology for using services to construct services and has two major focuses: (1) The creation of processes, operating in the form of services, to support both IT-enabled and non-IT-enabled business activities; and (2) The control and support of the business services through a formal process for managing services. To summarize, governance provides support for empowering people to do what they do in line with organizational objectives.

Orchestration

Orchestration refers to the dynamic linking of services together to achieve a business purpose. The business processes are layered on top of the services, so in a sense, the services are anchored into the processes. In IT-enabled processes, the business process is a script written in a "business process execution language" that successively calls the needed components in order to invoke the services constituting the business function. This combinatory operation was earlier referred to as composition and can be conceptualized as the workflow of services. In a non-IT enabled process, the composition is achieved through management directed policies, procedures, and business rules.

Actually, the term "orchestration" has two meanings in the context of service science. Let's take a computer application as an example. The first meaning has to do with setting up the structure as a controlling module that successively invokes services to achieve a business objective. The components do not have some form of inherent stickiness that enables operational affinity among loosely-coupled components in a meaningful order. That is where the business process execution language (BPEL), referred to just above, comes in. The application designer has to set up the service chain beforehand.

The service bus effectively connects the registry, workflow, composition, and the underlying system (called the *platform*) as pieces that do the work to construct function from components viewed as services. The second meaning of the term "orchestration" refers to the actual running of the application. The BPEL script is actually executed by an operational entity, intermediate data is stored in an operational database (not shown), and the business result is achieved.

Analysis

One of the facets of the service domain is that service quality is directly related to client interaction and involvement. This requires constant tweaking, otherwise known as continuous improvement (i.e., *kaizen* in operations management). Business performance is constantly monitored – there is nothing new about this. With service systems, however, the raw operational data is frequently embedded deep down in independently constructed loosely-coupled components. Getting this data out for analysis is a task that should be addressed at the design level.

User Interaction

On the surface, the end-user interface development model seems simple. All that needs to be done is to construct a prototype, test it, improve it, and then have the end-user group sign off on it. With service-oriented architecture, however, the *user interaction* is with a business process, which is a notch up from what normally is construed as the end-user interface. The term "user," therefore, refers to the user of a service, and not necessarily to the user of an application. As in the restaurant example, the user of a service doesn't have to be the customer.

The user of a service can be another service, which leads to the notion of a service architecture in which components can be assembled without the use of special adapters.

SERVICE ARCHITECTURE PRINCIPLES

The use of design principles is paramount to the construction of a successful service project. Otherwise, service systems development is another "random walk down Wall Street." Here is a set of service architecture principles.

Service Abstraction. The key benefit of service abstraction is that "inside" information about a component is effectively hidden from the outside so that a component can be used by other diverse services. This principle is sometimes referred to as information hiding. Often, internal operational details are superfluous to a referencing service where only a result is needed. Take the credit checking service as an example. An outside user of that service is usually only interested in the credit worthiness of a subject and not in the procedures and file processes necessary to ascertain that rating. In fact, operational details may change without the requester knowing or caring about them. The concept of abstraction applies to other organizational functions and computer modules, as well.

Service Encapsulation. Service encapsulation enables a service – often bundled as part of a larger operational entity – to be referenced via an adapter to preserve and take advantage of previously developed functionality. As with the preceding principle, encapsulation may apply to organizational as well as informational components.

Service Loose Coupling. This principle simply demands that

106

components are not implicitly dependent upon one another, such that use by a non-coupled component is prohibited. Another way of expressing the concept of loose coupling is one component does not require that another component be in a particular state at the time of invocation.

Service Contract. The concept of a service contract reflects that it is necessary that a complete specification be made of the precise services provided by a service component and exactly how those services are to be addressed. A service contract describes how two components are to interact. With Web services, the contract refers to a WSDL (Web Services Definition Language) definition and a specification of the XML schema definition of precisely how messages between a requester and the repository are to be formatted.

Service Reusability. Service reusability simply refers to the practice of designing a component so that it can be used in more than one place. In general, the intention is to provide services that can be used by more than one business process.

Service Composability. Service composability refers to the combining of services to form composite services. This practice implicitly imposes a restriction on the component services so that they adhere to the specifications in the service contract. Service composition is usually performed to synthesize a business process.

Service Autonomy. Service autonomy is conceptually modeled after the human nervous system and refers to a component's capability to self-govern its own operational behavior. Autonomy reduces the complexity of business processes composed from self-regulating components. Autonomy allows a business process to provide a higher level of productivity by being able to manage itself. This is a tricky principle, because the implication is that a component just operates on its own as some artificial intelligence robot. For most services, this principle simply means that a service invoked through some form of "service bus" takes its input parameters and performs its functions, as specified in its service contract, without requesting additional input or operating instructions.

Service Discoverability. Service discoverability is a complex arrangement of being describable, via the service contract, and being accessible via a registry and a description language. Essentially, this means that the description of a service, found through a search process, additionally provides information on how to use a service.

SERVICE ARCHITECTURE STRUCTURE AND OPERATION

A business process is composed of one or more business services frequently implemented through information and communications technology (ICT). Krafzig, Banke, and Slama state the modern dependence on ICT in the following way. "… enterprises heavily depend on the IT backbone, which is responsible for running almost all processes of modern enterprises, be they related to manufacturing, distribution, sales, customer management, accounting, or any other type of business process." This section introduces the concept of enterprise systems and then presents definitive information on the structure and operation of service architecture in an enterprise environment.

Enterprise Systems

An enterprise system cuts across the total organization and encompasses inter-departmental dependencies and relationships with suppliers and business partners. Accordingly, the enterprise software should be tightly coupled with the organization, but not with itself, based on the component model. This reflects the agility and incremental change that we referred to earlier. We require a structure that promotes loose coupling through messaging and platform interoperability.

Service Architecture Structure

The key structural elements in a service system are the services, a service repository, the service broker, the service bus, the service manager, and the interface elements. The interface elements can be to end users or to application programs.

From a structural viewpoint, the *service* provides business logic and consists of an implementation and a service contract. The *service repository*, operating as a virtual library, exists as a place to store service information and how to retrieve that information. The service repository certainly has a computer flavor to it, but that need not be the case. Many service firms have manual lists of the services they offer. In the computer version of a service repository, however, the storage facility could be accessed manually during development and dynamically during the execution of a component. The *service broker* connects services together by accessing the service repository for information about services and providing the linkage to connect components. The *service bus* is the nerve center in an enterprise system and is covered separately, as is the service manager, which is the mechanism by which enterprise processes are constructed. The interface elements are the input and output to the system.

The term "interface" normally implies an end-user interface with which most persons are familiar. In the case of enterprise systems, however, an interface can be to another computer application, a database, or a legacy system.

Enterprise Service Bus

An *enterprise service bus* (ESB) is a collection of ICT facilities for routing messages between services, or more specifically between components. The bus metaphor is apt in this case. The message gets on, goes to its destination, and gets off. The metaphor ends there, because there are different kinds of busses and unique things happen on different busses.

The most straightforward kind of service bus is a high-speed data link between services, as alluded to earlier in the stock broker example. The stock broker needs the current price of a stock for an ongoing transaction. The stock symbol is entered into a workstation and a button is pressed. In a fraction of a second, the current price is returned by a service connected to the other end of the service bus. The service bus in this instance, is a combination of hardware and software, often referred to as middleware. In this model of bus, the service bus could also be a specially constructed data link between business partners or between organizational units, termed electronic data interchange (EDI).

The most general form of ESB, however, uses the Internet with all of its inherent requirements for interoperability. In this instance, a message, perhaps requesting a service, may go through a necessary protocol conversion in its route from sender to receiver. Another possible function performed by an ESB is *context mediation*, which refers to a change in value based on contextual differences. An example would be the change of a price from Yen to Dollars during message processing.

Another related topic is *web based intermediary*, or WBI for short. A WBI is a program that runs in concert with a client's browser and acts as a form of software assistant, filtering and preparing information to satisfy particular needs.

Service Manager

The most prevalent use of service architecture is to construct computer applications. The service manager ties everything together and runs the show. Clearly, this is an operational function, but a structural component is needed to do it. In a sense, the service manager is the "main program" of an application. The service manager could be a specially written component in an enterprise system, or it could be a vendor-supplied package that successively calls upon required services.

Service Architecture Operation

An enterprise system is sometimes referred to as an "end to end" operation that represents a business process. Another means of conceptualizing an enterprise system is that it is controlled process flow. As covered above, the service manager controls the process flow through a process called *orchestration*. The conductor of an orchestra controls the activity of a set of musicians through minute actions termed orchestration. The same concept can be applied to the execution of an enterprise system.

Orchestration is different than choreography. Choreography refers to what a collection of services can do, and orchestration refers to precisely when and how they actually do it.

A business process can be scripted in a language, such as BPEL, or written in a computer programming language. Business Process Execution Language (BPEL) is an XML-based scripting language for orchestrating service applications.

QUICK SUMMARY

The purpose of this overview is to present a bird's eye view of service technology and architecture. The principles inherent in this viewpoint are summarized in the following quick summary.

1. Services are ubiquitous but require messages to communicate information between client and provider. A client and a provider can be tightly coupled, as when a patient is sitting in front of the doctor, and they are having a give-and-take conversation, or loosely coupled, as when you send a request to someone via email and receive a response at some undetermined time in the future. In the former case, the client and provider are communicating in a *synchronous mode* without technology, and in the latter case, they are communicating in an *asynchronous mode* with the use of technology.

2. The focus is on the data that is transmitted and not on the communications medium, which can take the form of a human interaction or a computer-based message. The context for the message can be embedded in the message or inherent in the way that the service provider is addressed. It is useful to recognize that we are operating at two levels: the service level and the message level. At the *service level*, the message entity that receives the message is the service provider, and in the case of a computer, it is regarded simply as the service. At the *message level*, there is some choreography involved with providing a service, as demonstrated by the above two-step interaction. In fact, a service may involve the interchange of several messages.

3. In its most simple form, a message is a string of characters encoded using standardized coding methods commonly employed in computer and information technology. Messages have a uniform format

consisting of a header and a body. The *header* primarily concerns addressing and includes the address of the sender and of the receiver. In the request/reply message pattern, the return address is picked up from the message header for the response portion of the transaction. The *body* of the message contains the information content of the message, and because it is intended only for the receiver, it is not usually inspected during message transmission.

4. A service that takes place on the Internet and the World Wide Web is called a *web service*. A web service is a process in which the provider and client interact to produce a value; it is a pure service. The only difference between a web service and medical provisioning, for example, is that, in the former case, the client and provider are computer systems. The most pervasive web service computer application on the Internet is electronic mail, commonly known as email. The most widely used application on the World Wide Web is to find information. The major web technology tools and techniques are HTTP, HTML, and XML.

5. *HyperText Transfer Protocol* (HTTP) is a collection of rules and procedures for transferring messages between computers over the World Wide Web. Without HTTP, the web would not be the revolutionary phenomena that it is today.

6. It is possible to send a document from one computer to another and have that document displayed on the receiving end in a reasonable form without regard to the brand and model of computer, kind of software, time of day, and location. This feat is possible because of hypertext markup language (HTML).

7. Extensible Markup Language (XML) is a language and a standard for service messaging. Whereas HTML describes how a document will be rendered on the receiving end of a message, XML gives the semantics (or meaning) of a document.

8. A Web Service is any service that is available over the Internet, uses a standard XML messaging system, and is not dependant upon any one particular operating system.

9. *Service architecture* is a collection of design patterns for constructing services from building blocks that can be shared between service systems. The basic idea behind service architecture is that you have a collection of components, representing business functions or

computer applications, and you want to fit them together to make a business process or an information system.

10. Components encapsulate services so that a service-oriented application or a business process is assimilated from multiple components that achieve the desired functionality by collectively orchestrating the operation of the needed services. The guiding principle behind service-oriented architecture is that once a component is established, it can be reused in other applications or business processes. Eventually, an organization runs out of components to build so that the synthesis of an application or a business process becomes a matter of piecing the components together.

11. The term "on demand" seems to have navigated its way into the business literature in at least three ways. In the first instance, on demand refers to the access of information, such as from the World Wide Web or any other information repository, from wherever the end user may be and whenever the interaction takes place. In the second instance, on demand refers to access to computer application programs without specifically having to purchase them. Also known as *utility computing*, this form of on demand would allow an end user to pay only for the use of software, rather than having to purchase it, as is typically the case with traditional office software. Finally, the third instance of on demand and the one in which we are interested refers to the techniques for the rapid development of business processes and computer information systems to support enterprise services.

12. It's all relatively straightforward: most components encapsulate one or more services; many complex services require more than one component; enterprise processes are constructed from components; and enterprise functions are an amalgamation of corresponding services. The notion of putting components together to achieve some enterprise function is called *composability*, and in order to do so, the methodology demands severe constraints on the manner in which the components are constructed and packaged for reuse. Components must fit together in order to operate as intended; this requirement is known as *interoperability*.

13. An enterprise is service oriented if it can be properly viewed as a set of services connected to produce a specific result. Similarly, a computer application or information system is service oriented if is constructed

from interacting components running on the same platform or accessible from different platforms via networking facilities.

14. Service architecture purports to leverage legacy systems by unlocking the business functionality through loosely-coupled but well-structured service components abducted from legacy systems. The service components can then be choreographed to adapt or extend business processes to satisfy current needs. This can be achieved in two ways: leveraging or repurposing. With *leveraging*, the functions in legacy systems are exposed without rewriting the system. With *repurposing*, the programs are rewritten for the modern world with a modern language, such as Java, for use on servers designed for the Internet and the World Wide Web. Clearly, leveraging is the way to go with legacy systems, because of the risk involved with rewriting large programs and getting it right the first time.

15. A certain amount of structure among components is required for the capabilities, mentioned above, to function together as a coherent whole. It is commonly known as the *SOA Reference Architecture*.

16. The use of design principles is paramount to the construction of a successful service project. A set of service architecture principles includes the following elements: service abstraction, service encapsulation, service loose coupling, service contract, service reusability, service composability, service autonomy, and service discoverability.

17. An enterprise system cuts across the total organization and encompasses inter-departmental dependencies and relationships with suppliers and business partners. Accordingly, the enterprise software should be tightly coupled with the organization, but not with itself, based on the component model. The key structural elements in a service system are the services, a service repository, the service broker, the service bus, the service manager, and the interface elements. The interface elements can be to end users or to application programs. An *enterprise service bus* (ESB) is a collection of ICT facilities for routing messages between services, or more specifically between components.

18. An enterprise system is sometimes referred to as an "end to end" operation that represents a business process. As covered above, the service manager controls the process flow through a process called *orchestration*. Orchestration is different than choreography. Choreography refers to what a collection of services can do, and

orchestration refers to precisely when and how they actually they do it.

REFERENCES

[1] Carter, S., The *New Language of Business*, Upper Saddle River, NJ: IBM Press, 2007.

[2] Cerami, E., *Web Services Essentials*, Sebastopol, CA: O'Reilly Media, Inc., 2002.

[3] Cherbakov, L., Galambos, G., Harishankar, R., Kalyana, S., and G. Rackham, "Impact of service orientation at the business level," *IBM Systems Journal*, Vol. 44, No. 4, 2005, pp. 653-668.

[4] Dykes, L. and E. Tittel, *XML for Dummies* (4th Edition), Hoboken, NJ: Wiley Publishing, Inc. 2005.

[5] Erl, T., *Service-Oriented Architecture: A Field Guide to Integrating XML and Web Services*, Upper Saddle River, NJ: Prentice Hall, 2004.

[6] Erl, T., *SOA: Principles of Service Design*, Upper Saddle River, NJ: Prentice Hall, 2008.

[7] Ernest, M. and J.M. Nisavic, "Adding value to the IT organization with the Component Business Model, *IBM Systems Journal*, Vol. 46, No. 3, 2007, provider.387-403.

[8] Gottschalk, K., Graham, S., Kreger, H., and J. Snell, "Introduction to Web services architecture," *IBM Systems Journal* (Vol. 41, No. 2), 2002, pp 170-177.

[9] Hagel, J. and J.S. Brown, *The Only Sustainable Edge*, Boston: Harvard Business School Press, 2007.

[10] Hurwitz, J., Bloor, R., Baroudi, C., and M. Kaufman, *Service Oriented Architecture for Dummies*, Hoboken, NJ: Wiley Publishing, Inc., 2007.

[11] IBM Corporation, *Extend the value of your core business systems: Transforming legacy applications into an SOA framework*, Form G507-1950-00, September 2006.

[12] Katzan, H. "Foundations of Service Science: Technology and Architecture," *Journal of Service Science*, 2(1): 11-33, 2009.

[13] Krafzig, D., Banke, K., and D. Slama, *Enterprise SOA: Service-Oriented Architecture Best Practices*, Upper Saddle River, NJ: Prentice Hall, 2005.

[14] Margolis, B. with J. Sharpe, *SOA for the Business Developer: Concepts, BPEL, and SCA*, Lewisville, TX: 2007.

[15] McGrath, M., *XML in Easy Steps*, New York: Barnes & Noble Books, 2003.

[16] Musciano, C. and B. Kennedy, *HTML: The Definitive Guide*, Sebastopol, CA: O'Reilly Media, Inc., 1998.

[17] Potts, S. and M. Kopack, *Web Services in 24 Hours*, Indianapolis: Sams Publishing, 2003.

[18] Smith, J., *Inside Windows Communication Foundation*, Redmond, WA: Microsoft Press, 2007.

[20] Spohrer, J., *Service Science, Management, and Engineering (SSME): State of the Art – service science*, IBM Nordic Service Science Summit, Helsinki, Finland, February 28, 2007.

[21] Van Slyke, C. and F. Bélanger, *E-Business Technologies: Supporting the Net-Enhanced Organization*, New York: John Wiley and Sons, Inc., 2003.

[22] Watt, A., *Teach Yourself XML in 10 Minutes*, Indianapolis: Sams Publishing, 2003.

[23] webMethods, *SOA Reference Architecture: Defining the Key Elements of a Successful SOA Technology Framework*, www.webMethods.com, 2006.

[24] Wikipedia, *HTTP*, www.wikipedia.org, 2007.

[25] Woods, D. and T. Mattern, *Enterprise SOA: Designing IT for Business Innovation*, Sebastopol, CA: O'Reilly Media Inc., 2006.

***** End of Essay 5 *****

6

SERVICE PRINCIPLES

SERVICE CONCEPTS

The basic concepts of service, service systems, and service science have been well-developed. (Sampson and Froehle 2006, Maglio and Zysman 2007, and Katzan 2008b) To fully benefit from the service perspective, however, an ontological foundation is required to facilitate communication among researchers and assist with the ongoing theoretical and pragmatic development of the discipline. To some extent, an ontology is dependent upon a particular point of view, and this paper seeks to identify a set of rigid descriptors that are linked to the various underlying concepts. We are going to take the view that a comprehensive depiction of the application domain is as important in service ontology as is the taxonomy used to describe it.

Service

In a widely distributed paper on the science of service, Spohrer and associates (Spohrer 2007b) give several characteristics of an elementary service event: customer participation, simultaneity, perishability, intangibility, and heterogeneity. *Customer participation* refers to the co-production of the service experience and the co-creation of service value. *Simultaneity* denotes the fact that a service is produced and consumed simultaneously. *Perishability* refers to time perishable capacity from the provider's viewpoint and opportunity loss from the client's perspective. *Intangibility* normally denotes the obvious fact that goods are not produced by a service event. Lastly, *heterogeneity* refers to the variation in a service from client to client and from provider to provider, along with the recognition that a service system is a complex system that can be mediated by information technology. This seemingly simple definition belies the complexity of the situation, since there is a multiplicity of service definitions, based on existential considerations. A service is a socially constructed temporal event, and within that domain, an objectivist view of the subject matter is adopted. Service exists and possesses an implicit lifecycle comprised of design, development, analysis, and implementation, similar in nature to most technical innovations. Specificity will be added to the service lifecycle model in a later section. Moreover, a service evolves and is subject to descriptive and nominative modalities. As with traditional social activities, a service can be analyzed and measured. In fact, a service is an economic entity that possesses demonstrable value to the participants, in particular, and to organizations and society, as a whole.

Services are indigenous to the existence of modern society. In fact, if one replaces the concept of labor with that of service, the principles of service science can be derived from the essential work of Adam Smith (Smith 1776), most pointedly in his notions of "value in use" and "value in exchange."

Social Constructivism

Social constructivism is a theory of knowledge (epistemology) based, at least in part, on the social and material setting in which a belief is produced or maintained. In social constructivism, individuals and groups participate in a perceived reality, and create an element of knowledge, as espoused by the philosophical doctrine of Equal Validity. (Boghossian 2006, Bergquist 1993) Equal validity suggests the notion that other means of knowing exist in addition to the factual predominance of scientific investigation. Consider an example of a simple wooden chair developed in antiquity and regarded as a place to sit and pile books. A chair is made from a type of wood that we, as a society, have discovered as being useful to the purpose. Wood exists as a natural phenomenon independently of chairs and the social setting in which it exists. The precise form and substance of a chair, however, is a socially constructed form of knowledge that none but the hardened skeptic would deny is a valid form of knowledge. Service systems are socially constructed forms of interaction wherein entities exchange beneficial forms of action through the combination of people and technologies that adapt to the changing level of information in the system. As such, reality constructed through social mechanisms is a dynamic process replicated and maintained by social interactions within a service and between services.

Service systems are actual social phenomena that existed, in part, before the development of service science and are analogous to economic systems that existed before the development and study of economics. Both types of systems are governed by events in their operational environments and are continually being created, modified, and retired. A service is neither synthetic (like synthetic rubber or various chemical compounds) nor artificial (like artificial intelligence in the computer field). Services are observable, and through a process of shared reality, concepts are developed that lead to classes of service and subsequently instances of that service. We are going to apply epistemological concepts to develop a service ontology that adheres to the hypothetico-deductive modality of scientific research. (Sutherland 1975)

Service Universe

A *service universe* is a collection of services under consideration at a given point in time by a person, group, organization, or even a society. A service universe is typically a set of services, organized in some fashion to achieve a discernable purpose. However, that need not necessarily be the case, and could be a disparate collection of temporal service events, or even a combination of the two categories. The notion of a service is problematical, because there are differing points of view on exactly what constitutes a service, even though most persons could reliably identify a service when confronted with one. Professional, technical, and scientific people are service providers, even though they do not normally think of themselves in that fashion. Call centers, consulting companies, and utilities also do service, but dry cleaners and fast-food restaurants do them, as well. The subject is important because 80-90% of the working population in developed countries is engaged in services, and they are also consumers of services.

A simple question on this subject, such as "What is a service?' can yield a surprisingly large number of different answers. Here are a few instances that would immediately come to mind:

1. An action performed by one person or group on behalf of another person, organization, or group.
2. A generic type of action, such as a medical service or a web service.
3. The process of performing some action classified as a service.
4. The result of an action – typically a change affecting an object or person.
5. The utility of a change affecting a person or object – the value proposition.
6. An organization behaving in a prescribed way to benefit or operate in the best interests of a person or group.
7. A promise, contractual agreement, or obligation to perform a specified action in the future as a response to a triggering event.
8. The deployment of service assets for the benefit of service participants, commonly regarded as provider and client.

There are two fundamentally different points of view: the global view and the local view. The *global view* refers to the notion of a system comprised of interacting and complementary services. One could consider the global view as an external service description, useful for determining how a collection of services functions in order to benefit various people, organizations, and business processes. This view is analogous to macroeconomics. The *local view* describes and delineates the steps in a distinct service process, emphasizing the service participants and the complementary roles they play in the service event. This view is analogous to microeconomics. A discrete service fits nicely into one of several mutually exclusive categories based on service characteristics that can be distinguished with a service DNA. (Katzan 2008a) In this paper, we are going to adopt global and local viewpoints and structure the ontology according to that dichotomy. Between the global and local points-of-view, we are going to develop a consistent set of underlying concepts, relationships, and language elements.

Service Systems

A singular service event is a form of social organization in which two or more resources interact to achieve an agreed-upon purpose, where a resource can be a person, organization, or an element of technology. The service is the unit of exchange in the interaction that is established to produce value for each of the participants. (Spohrer 2007b) The resources are commonly referred to as service entities or, simply, entities. Based on this assessment, we can propose the following definition:

Definition of Service Two entities collaborate and what is produced from the interaction is a service, *if and only if*

- Both parties participate in the exchange
- Both parties benefit from the exchange such that value is co-created in a complementary form
- The action of the service is complementary
- The parties assume complementary but differing roles
- The roles are commonly known as *provider* and *client.*

The provider role is regarded as a serving activity, and the client role is, similarly, regarded as a receiving activity. Moreover, the collaboration adapts to the win-win model of economic exchange, since value is co-created for both participants. The complementary form of activity is intended to distinguish it from a supplementary form in which participants operate as partners to perform a stated function. For example, a physician and a patient exhibit complementary roles in a service, whereas a scenario in which two masons work together to build a structure represents a supplementary form of behavior. A singular service event is the most elementary form of a service system. (Spohrer 2007)

A unified service is a process that takes input and produces output. In between the input and the output, there exists one or more steps that constitute the service process. (Sampson and Froehle 2006, Katzan 2008) The steps in a service process often include other services leading to the concept of a service system.

A *service system* is a collection of resources, economic entities, and other services capable of engaging in and supporting one or more service events. Services, i.e., service processes, may interact or they may be included in a service value chain. This is a recursive definition of a service system that would support the following modalities of service operation: *tell me, show me, help me, and do it for me.* Service systems are inherently multidisciplinary, since a service provider may not have the knowledge, skill, time, resources, and inclination to perform all of the steps in a service process and, thus, require the services of an external service provider.

As introduced above, service systems are social constructs that commonly encompass other services and are components of a larger reality. An organizational structure of this particular genre could be regarded from either of two points of view: as an economy or as an adaptive social structure. As an *economy*, it is a system of relationships that govern the availability of scarce resources and operate under conditions of efficiency and effectiveness. As an *adaptive social structure,* the efficacy of a service event depends upon the dynamic environment in which an organization operates. (Selznick 1948) A service system is a cooperative dynamically changing formal system, with a porous boundary so that the environment it which it resides has a deterministic effect on its behavior.

A unified service system requires some sort of organizational entanglement so that an enterprise can invest prudently and produce predictable outcomes. Accordingly, research into the mechanics of service systems requires three things: an appropriate operational platform, a design theoretic formulation, and an ontology of service and service systems, which is introduced in subsequent sections.

Service Science

With regard to academic disciplines, there is an old saying that goes somewhat as follows: "If it has the word 'science' in its title, then it isn't science." It would appear that service science is an exception. There are two fundamental questions: "What is science, anyway?" and "What does a conceptualization of science have to do with service?"

In an earlier debate concerning computer science, Newell, Perlis, and Simon (Newell 1967) state, "Wherever there are phenomena, there can be a science to describe and explain those phenomena." Further, Kuhn (Kuhn 1962) states, "Science is the agreed upon methods and standards of rigor used by a community to develop a body of knowledge that accounts for observable phenomenon with conceptual frameworks, theories, models, and laws that can be empirically tested and applied within a world view or paradigm." Moreover, since service systems are an observable and evolving phenomena, subject to the dynamics of the economic world, the development of a science of service, replete with its own frameworks, models, and theories, is an essential element in a total world view. (Spohrer 2007a)

Epistemologically, there exists a conceptual service universe in which observable services and service systems operate. One can view this service universe in a manner similar to the way in which we view the physical universe described by physics and chemistry. The modus operandi in those disciplines is to abstract a piece of that universe and study it as a sub-discipline. Mechanics, heat, and sound are elementary sub-disciplines that fall into the discipline of physics.

The services in the service universe can be viewed metaphorically as entities floating around in a service space waiting for the chance to be called upon to execute as a singular event, as a component of a service system, or as a chance to be called upon interactively. Some services are used in more than one service system. *Service science* is a collection of models of sub-disciplines abstracted from the service universe, in much the same manner that the physical sciences are collections of sub-disciplines. The procedure in all cases is to take a piece of an existing system and put it under the microscope of academic scrutiny. Thus, a particular service or a service system is an abstraction of service science, as with the physical universe, and a service theory is a means of tying the various models together. On the other hand, if one views the entire amorphous service space as a service system, then service science could be alternately viewed as a basic abstraction of service systems, realizing, of course, that the ultimate objective is to study categories of service systems.

There are, of course, additional considerations regarding the phenomena of service and service systems. Services evolve and are continually being developed and modified. Service systems are affected through their porous boundaries by stakeholders, laws, and social customs. They also require formalization as important aspects of the discipline of service science.

ONTOLOGY

Ontology is a specification of "what is." In philosophy, use of the term reflects the study of being (or existence) and describes and delineates a collection of basic categories, and defines the entities and classes of elements within a category. In service science, ontology is a specification of a conceptualization used to enable knowledge sharing. Since ontology concerns existence, an ontological definition of a subject – perhaps a service category – reflects a materialization of a concept obtained through a shared reality, and not what it is called or how it is made or used. In this paper, the definition of ontology, as "a set of representational primitives with which to model a domain of knowledge or discourse," will be adopted. (Gruber 2008, Wikipedia 2009a) More specifically, ontology can be viewed as a data model that describes objects, classes, attributes, and relations. In his ground-breaking book on knowledge representation, John F. Sowa gives an appropriate definition for our purposes:

> The subject of *ontology* is the study of the *categories* of things that exist or may exist in some domain. The product of such a study, called *ontology*, is a catalog of the types of things that are assumed to exist in a domain of interest *D* from the perspective of a person who uses the language *L* for the purpose of talking about *D*. The types in the ontology represent the *predicates, word senses,* or *concept and relation types* of the language *L* when used to discuss topics in the domain *D*. (Sowa 2000)

One common approach to the delineation of ontological elements is to divide the extant entities into groups called "categories." These lists of categories can be quite different from one another. It is in this latter sense that ontology is applied to such fields as theology, service science, and artificial intelligence. (Wikipedia 2009)

Ontological Naming

In the naming of ontological elements, it is important to note that there are two approaches to the use of nouns. In one philosophical school, nouns should refer to existent entities. In the alternate school, nouns are used as a shorthand as reference to a collection of objects or events. For example the word *mind* would refer to a collection of mental states, and society would refer to a collection of people.

Ontological Engineering

Ontological engineering encompasses a set of activities conducted during conceptualization, design, implementation, and deployment of ontologies.

(Dedvedzic 2002) Ontological engineering seeks to achieve the following goals in a given domain:

Definition of terms
Establishment of a body of domain knowledge
Specification of coherent and expressive knowledge bases

In short, ontology defines the vocabulary of a problem domain and a set of constraints on how terms are related. It also gives data types and operations defined over the data types.

Most forms of ontology are expressed in an ontologic language and share structural similarities, such as individuals, classes, attributes, relations, function, restrictions, rules, axioms, and events. The basic idea behind ontology languages is to allow software agents to communicate in a knowledge intensive computer-based environment: We are going to concentrate on the following components: (Guarino 1995, Wikipedia 2009)

Individuals referring to instances and objects
Classes expressed as sets, collections, and kinds of things
Attributes giving features and characteristics of individuals and classes
Relations that determine ways that individuals and classes relate

The components determine whether a specific ontology is a domain ontology or an upper ontology. In a *domain ontology*, a specific type would be relevant to a particular category, such as in a medical or household category. In an *upper ontology*, a type would be applicable to all ontologies in the universe of discourse. In the service ontology, presented in the following section, we are going to be developing an upper ontology for service systems.

UPPER ONTOLOGY FOR SERVICE SYSTEMS

The ontology of service systems is a developmental artifact for the study, design, analysis, and application of services. Essentially, a framework is needed to tie the elements together, so that they are applicable to a wide range of operational scenarios. (Alter 2008) The primary measure of an ontological determination is how it assists in delineating the value chain for services, comprised of people, technology, and organizations, and its relevance to education, government, business, and other social phenomena.

Service Systems Lifecycle

Service science is one of the few disciplines in which the basic principles and resultant theory apply to both small-scale and large-scale operations. We are going to proceed with that assumption. In its most basic form, a service is a value producing interaction between a service provider and a service client, consisting of a process conceptualized as a layered set of activities. (Ferrario and Guardino 2008) It is useful to conceptualize the layers according to the following global service system lifecycle:

Service commitment
Service production
Service availability
Service delivery
Service analysis
Service termination

Initially, we are going to be looking at services from a global viewpoint, where the lifecycle pertains to a set of generic services supplied by an economic entity, such as a governing body, a business, an institution, or an individual acting in a service capacity. *Service commitment* refers to the formal agreement to provide a class of services to a service audience by a principal or trustee with the proper administrative control over the service environment. The agreement to provide fire service by a municipality and the founding of a health clinic are common examples. *Service production* pertains to service provisioning, infrastructure, availability, quality management, and back-office processing. The producer is the agent of the principal in a prototypical principal-agent scenario. The principal and agent may be the same economic entity or different economic entities depending upon the scope of the service domain. The manager of a chain of restaurants and the medical director of a clinic are examples. *Service availability* is the time during which a service is available. Commitment does not necessarily imply availability, because of a variety of spatiotemporal events. *Service delivery* is the class of actions usually regarded as the service and is the layer where the service client comes into the picture. The doctor/patient relationship is a good example of this layer. The service provider, who could have a dual role as producer, is an agent of the producer as the primary source of service revenue and the primary provider of a service. *Service analysis* refers to measurement activities and the determination of value propositions needed to sustain service operations. *Service termination* reflects the inevitable consequence of a dynamic and evolving economic environment where a total service operation has to be retired, because of insufficient activity or realigned opportunities. The global lifecycle represents a provisioning perspective of service systems.

Service Entities

We are looking at five service entities: the *service principal*, functioning as a trustee of a service or a service system; the *service producer*, responsible for the availability, infrastructure, service provisioning, and back-office processing; the *service provider*, charged with the application of resources for the benefit of another service entity; the *service client*, who has a complementary service relationship with the service provider; and the *service object* that may be the direct recipient of the result of the service process.

A *service entity* need not be a person, but can be a group, organization, business, governing body, educational institution, or a physical object, such as a possession or an element of computer software.

Service Commitment

Service commitment is a guarantee by a principal to provide a set of actions that constitutes a service. A common example might be the promise of a mayor of a town to provide fire service to his constituents. (Ferrario and Guardino 2008) The principal can be an organization, such as a government, a medical group, an educational institution, a private service business, a consulting firm with a service-level agreement, or an ad hoc entity that provides service to other service entities. A service commitment may result from an explicit declaration, such as "I agree to provide said service to a receiving agent" or be implicit in a legal charter or understanding, such as a medical practice or financial institution. A service commitment may apply to all constituents in the principal's domain – perhaps to all families moving into a community or entering a service facility.

The committed service may not, and probably will not, be performed by the principal, who may rely on a service producer and an ensuing service provider known as a *service agent* to actually execute the service process. Thus, a service agent provides a service to the principal and to the service object. The service principal, producer, and provider may coincide or be distinct to some degree.

Service Production

Service production supports a service commitment by establishing service parameters, such as time, location, availability, infrastructure, provisioning, record keeping, and legal compliance and certification. Time and location are key factors in service delivery that are summarized through a service DNA, which partitions the service domain into mutually exclusive service categories. (Katzan 2008a) The principle element in service production is maintenance of the service infrastructure, consisting of physical facilities, operational procedures, satisfaction of legal requirements, competent provider provisioning, and dependable auxiliary service provisioning.

Service Availability

The *availability* of a service is dependent upon the inherent nature of the service commitment. The access to and duration of medical provisioning, banking, insurance, product warranties, and household service, as examples, probably differ in most cases. It is important to additionally note the significance of service commitment with regard to service availability. What a service principal commits to is the *service content* and not to its associated service process, scheduling, and other operational considerations.

Service Delivery

In order for a service provider and a client to co-create a service event, there must be some degree of locality to the situation, in the sense that the client travels to the provider, the provider travels to the client, the client and provider execute the service event in a third-party location, or they communicate via some form of interactive device and its corresponding media. Location is basic to service provisioning. When the client travels to the provider site, the location is termed a *service factory* and the client or the service object remain in the service factory for the duration of the service transaction. When the service object is left in the provider's facilities, the location is known as a *service shop*. The provider may travel to *client facilities*, as in the cases of custodial work or nursing home care. With information service, the provider may reside in a remote facility and provide access through a service portal.

A related consideration is the distinction between *discrete service* and *continuous service*. There are many edge cases. Insurance is commonly regarded as a continuous service, as is banking – except in the cases where the customer visits a bank branch. Medical provisioning, automobile maintenance, and household service are usually regarded as discrete services. In the latter case, when a service event is over, it's over. A follow-on service is regarded as another service event.

Service Analysis

To some extent, all services consist of the application of resources, and the success of those services is dependent upon how efficiently and effectively those resources are applied in a normative manner to a specific problem domain. (Spohrer 2007a) Thus, measurement and analysis is required to assess both individual service interactions and the cumulative result of a set of service interactions. The basic tenet of service delivery is the following. *The client starts out with expectations, and a service deliverer should start out off by assessing what those expectations are.* However, not all service events are successful, so that a risk analysis should be performed by the providers and the client prior to a service engagement. In service analysis, the success of a service event is dependent upon how accurately the service providers and the client assess their roles.

Measurement and analysis are often the modus for judging service and service quality, and in an organizational setting, are achieved through service level agreements between complementary economic entities. For instances where implicit agreements persist, service analysis involves responsiveness, timeliness, and completeness – traditional metrics that have evolved through informal agreement.

Service Termination

In order for a service system to be successful, it must *exist* and *persist*. To exist, that service must satisfy the economic goals of provider, client, producer, and trustee in due consideration of the needs surrounding its competitors, partners (business or operational), employees, and investors. (Spohrer 2007a) The economic goals are known as the *value proposition* of the service consisting of the provider's sacrifice, the client's sacrifice, provider's exploitation, and the client's exploitation, from both short-term and long-term perspectives. (Alter 2008) Accordingly, a discrete service offering can be unsuccessful in either of four ways: (Spohrer op cit.)

> The client does not accept the provider's value proposition in light of his own.
> The client decides to engage in "self service'
> The client decides to accept service from an alternate source
> The client decides to forgo service

Thus, cumulative service decisions from within the *client domain* essentially determine the persistence of a service commitment.

DOMAIN ONTOLOGY FOR SERVICE

A discrete service event entails the commitment of resources for the benefit of a client. Each service event – frequently referred to as a service interaction – consists of a series of steps called *the service process* intended to achieve a particular goal. Within a given service category, the various service processes are similar within acceptable limits of variability.

Basic Service Categories

A *service* is a provider/client relationship (Katzan 2008b) that captures value for both participants that can be individuals, organizations, software, or a complex arrangement of the three. Service operations are customarily grouped into three classes: people processing, possession processing, and information processing. Within each domain, it is therefore important to view the client/provider relationship along the following dimensions:

Tangible vs. intangible
Primary vs. secondary
Facilitating vs. auxiliary

This approach focuses on the fact that a service event is a process consisting of primary and secondary services. (Sampson and Froehle 2006)

TANGIBLE AND INTANGIBLE SERVICE A *tangible service* is a provider/client event that results in demonstrable values to the service participants. With an individual service participant, this is a left-brain function (LBF). In retailing, it is the acquisition of a product including attendant activities that change the ownership attribute of the associated product. However, the value proposition for a product may be determined from the service it provides, rather than from the intrinsic value of its specific components. In pure service, such as a people and possession processing service, value is created through the work performed on behalf of the client by the provider. With information service, the service's value is derived from the transfer of information from service provider to the client. An *intangible service* provides value for a service participant through the perspective of a right-brain function (RBF). Certain products, such as premium automobiles (Rosengarten 2006), special jewelry, and elegant real estate, for example, are typically associated with a high-level of intangible service. As mentioned previously, the intangible value of a product may exceed its tangible value.

PRIMARY AND SECONDARY SERVICE A *primary service* is the core service for which the provider and the client interact to produce demonstrable value. Simple examples are a dental appointment or a lawn care service. A *secondary service* is a service that does not exist separately as a primary service and plays a supportive role to a primary service. Common examples are the weigh in and blood pressure checks associated with a doctor's visit and the acceptance and delivery of garments at a dry cleaning establishment. Secondary service can also exist as a supplementary or referral service.

FACILITATING AND AUXILIARY SERVICE A *facilitating service* is disjoint from a primary or secondary service and enables a client to obtain utility from a tangible service. Usability service, commonly associated with automobiles and computers, is a common example of a facilitating service. Another common example of a facilitating service is the purchase of an event ticket. In this instance, the event – be it a visit to the theatre, a sporting match, or an amusement park – is the tangible service and the ticket is the intangible service. An *auxiliary service* is independent from a core service and may be experienced before or after the primary service. A blood test taken prior to a doctor's appointment and a medical referral are examples of auxiliary services.

SERVICE FUNCTIONS Many service functions relate to satisfaction models for consumer judgments regarding service interactions. One of two possible viewpoints is selected: expectation confirmation or rational utility assessment. With the expectation confirmation approach, the psychological distance between expectation and realization is measured. The tangible aspects of service are emphasized. With the rational utility approach, the tangible factors of service delivery, as well as the intangible factors, are taken into consideration. *Tangible assessment* is a means of referring to the demonstrable attributes of service delivery, such as product characteristics, skills of the service provider, and explicit service results as they pertain to people, possession, and information processing service. Tangible service results are utilitarian and measurable. *Intangible assessment* is a means of referring to the feeling that one experiences from a service interaction or the ownership of a product. Intangible service results are affective and hedonistic. The level of intangible service is normally a function of the feelings that one derives from ownership of a premium product or the participation in a service event with a particular service provider. The service functions are summarized in the DNA of a category of service, presented in the appendix and covered below.

Service Process Lifecycle

It is necessary to identify the key events in the operational service lifecycle and the major entities involved. The *service lifecycle* can be viewed as those activities that exist between service acquisition and service termination – from both structural and operational viewpoints. From the *structural* point-of-view, the set of layered activities incorporate the service commitment, service infrastructure, service availability, service delivery, and the eventual termination of a service, as delineated previously for the upper service ontology. From an *operational* point-of-view, the layered activities describe service events and incorporate those transactable actions that constitute the essence of service.

Based on the above definitions, the lifecycle of a service process consists of a loosely defined set of steps intended to co-create value for complementary service participants. It is useful to conceptualize a generic lifecycle for a domain ontology as consisting of the following steps:

Service acquisition
Service invocation
Service execution
Service termination

Service acquisition refers to the process of identifying a service provider with the requisite infrastructure, and its corollary, the process of attracting clients. *Service invocation* involves the scheduling and logistics part of the service process. *Service execution* entails the actual steps in the service process including supplementary services. *Service termination* incorporates referral, warranty, and archiving activities. The requisite infrastructure for sustaining the service process lifecycle is referred to as the *service platform* and is related to the activities of the producer in the upper ontology, covered previously. The service process lifecycle can be viewed as a set of layered events. We are going to supplement the service process lifecycle with service analytics that are descriptive of the end state of a service event.

Service Acquisition

The generic steps that comprise service acquisition represent the handshaking needed to establish a service relationship. From the client perspective, acquisition consists of an awareness that some form of service is needed, known as *service awareness*, followed by the discovery of a suitable delivery vehicle, called *service discovery*, perhaps using Web Services, and finally the development of a service level agreement, usually known as *service negotiation*. From the provider perspective, service acquisition is fueled by a service commitment, service availability, and a variety of service conditions incorporated in the DNA of that service category. Prototypical examples of service acquisition are finding a doctor in a new town or locating a shop for automobile repair.

In a discrete service, the service provider assumes the role of the "service producer" and the service client assumes the role of the "service requestor," in the sense that the client takes the initiative in the acquisition process. In professional and technical services, the service provider often assumes the role of the requestor by directly approaching from a business perspective or through direct advertising.

Service Invocation

An exogenous condition is needed to initiate a service process by the service provider on behalf of a service client. (Ferrario 2008) It is termed a *triggering event* that can take one of a variety of forms, such as:

- An independent event requiring attention, such as a medical situation or a fire
- A request by the client, or its representative, to have a service performed that the client doesn't want to do, can't do, or the provider can do more efficiently
- A required service, perhaps by law or convention, initiated by the client or a governing body

The triggering event is typically followed by a *service scheduling* process that establishes a spatiotemporal location for service delivery. Some service providers use appointments to manage demand as a means of achieving service efficiency. The steps that facilitate core or primary service invocation are customarily regarded as a secondary service.

Service invocation involves back-office administrative record keeping and coordination, such that the provider and client can interact on a planned basis. The service delivery, availability, and demand dimensions of the service DNA sequence reflect the dynamics between provider and client in a service event. Appointments with professional service providers are formally scheduled, whereas arrangements with nonprofessionals are commonly scheduled on an informal basis.

Service Execution

Service execution is the phase of the service process lifecycle where the service provider engages the service client to achieve a goal state that reflects both provider and client perspectives. Alternately, the service object may be a service entity over which the client has legal or social responsibility. In general, the service object can be a person, a possession, information, or an abstract entity such as a financial investment. We are going to refer to the provider, the client, and the service object as *service participants*.

The primary objective of a service event is referred to as the *core service* that has tangible value to the service participants. The core service is conventionally comprised of primary, secondary, and auxiliary services, as described earlier under Basic Service Categories. We are going to establish five categories with which the execution of a service event, per se, can be determined:

Category	Alternative
Modality	discrete, continuous
Diversity	heterogeneous, homogeneous
Temporality	active, passive
Complexity	low complexity, high complexity
Duration	short, long

Modality denotes whether the texture of the service takes place as a single interaction (*discrete*), such as a doctor's visit that is over when it is over, or it takes place over an extended period of time (*continuous*), such as an insurance policy. *Diversity* refers to whether the service can be performed by a specific provider (*heterogeneous*), such as particular attorney or accountant, or any one of a group of providers (*homogeneous*), such as a bank teller. *Temporality* specifies whether the service is one in which the provider and client actively participate (*active*), such as a dentist's visit, or one in which the service participants are not actively engaged (*passive*) until a triggering event occurs, such as an insurance policy or a municipality's fire service. *Complexity* refers to whether the service is completed in a few similar steps (*low complexity*), or many different steps (*high complexity*). A hospital procedure or a home remodeling would reflect a high complexity; an appointment at the eye doctor's or a car detailing would exhibit low complexity. *Duration*, not to be confused with modality, refers to whether the service execution takes place in a few hours or less (*short duration*), or whether it takes place over a few days or longer (*high duration*). In medicine, a doctor's visit would have short duration, and a hospital stay would have long duration. In transportation, a ferry ride would have short duration, and a trans-Atlantic cruise would have long duration. Clearly, the collection of categories is generic and reflects the underlying difficulty in attempting to be specific with a ubiquitous social phenomena, such as service.

It is important to state the difference between DNA dimensions (see the *Appendix*) and categories of service execution. DNA dimensions are intended to describe and delineate the total service environment from the standpoint of upper and domain ontology. The categories of service execution are simply intended to provide specificity to the service process.

Service Termination and Analytics

Service termination and analytics encompass follow-on activity, record keeping, archiving, and the financial aspects of service. Accordingly, this essential lifecycle element involves both front-office and back-office activities on the part of the provider and the client, leading to quality and value assessments.

The service value analysis involves four components: provider's costs, provider's revenue, client's cost, client's revenue – recognizing that cost and revenue are not necessarily monetary. The *fundamental theorem of service delivery* applies to service analytics such that the cost of service by the provider must equal the value of commensurate service to the client, represented as:

$$C_p = V_C$$

where C_p is the cost to the provider and V_C is the value to the client. Accordingly,

$$C_p = C_p + C_s + C_t$$

where C_p is the cost of primary core service, C_s is the cost of secondary service, and C_t are the transaction costs.

Similarly,

$$V_C = V_t + V_i$$

where V_t is the value of tangible service and V_i is the value of intangible service.

Analytics help the provider and the client answer fundamental questions, such as: Should we? (*business value*), Can we? (*technology*), May we? (*governance*), and Will we? (*business priority*).

TAXONOMY OF SERVICE SYSTEMS

This section delineates a taxonomy of service systems. A taxonomy essentially provides a prose glossary of a body of knowledge and a methodology for systems analysis and design. In this particular instance, the taxonomy of service systems supplies a lens into a collection of concepts, definitions, and relations that describe the complex subject of service science.

1. Service Identification
   1.1 Service name
   1.2 Sponsoring organization
   1.3 Service initiation date
2. Service Participants
   2.1 Service principal
   2.2 Service producer
   2.3 Service provider
   2.4 Service client
   2.5 Service object
3. Service System Lifecycle
   3.1 Service commitment
   3.2 Service production
   3.3 Service availability
   3.4 Service delivery
   3.5 Service analysis
   3.6 Service termination
4. Service Process
   4.1 Service acquisition
      4.1.1 Service awareness
      4.1.2 Service discovery
      4.1.3 Service negotiation

In using the taxonomy of service systems, a service analyst would necessarily supply entries for each of the ontological elements, as required by a particular service system under investigation.

SUMMARY

An ontological introduction to the principles of service systems has been presented with an emphasis on concepts, classes, objects, relations, and terminology. This essay introduces social constructivism, as a basis of service science, and continues with service concepts, service systems, ontology, and then on to upper ontology for services, domain ontology for service, and finally a taxonomy of service systems, as well as a short treatise on a DNA of service.

REFERENCES

[1]   Alter. S. 2008. Service system fundamentals: Work system, value chain, and life cycle. *IBM System Journal*, 47(1): 71-85.

[2]   Bergquist, W. 1993. Post Modern Thought in a Nutshell. [Published in *Classics of Organization Theory* (4th Edition – J. Shafritz and J. Ott, editors), New York: Harcourt Brace College Publishers, 1996. Adapted from Bergquist, W. 1993. *The Postmodern Organization: Mastering the Art of Irreversible Change*, Jossey-Bass Inc., Publishers, pp. 15-36.]

[3]   Boghossian, P. 2006. *Fear of Knowledge: Against Relativism and Constructivism*. Oxford: Oxford University Press.

[4]   Dedvedzic, V. 2002. Understanding Ontological Engineering. *Communications of the ACM* 45(4):136-144.

[5]   Ferrario, R. and N. Guardino. 2008. Towards an Ontological Foundation for Services Science. *Proceedings of the Future Internet Symposium,* Vienna Austria, 28-30 September 2008.

[6]   Fitzsimmons, J.A. and M.J. Fitzsimmons. 2006. *Service Management: Operations, Strategy, Information Technology* (5th Edition), New York: McGraw-Hill Irwin.

[7]   Gruber, T. 2008. Ontology. *Encyclopedia of Database Systems*, Liu, L. and M. Ozsu (Eds.), Springer-Verlag,

[8]   Guarino, N. 1995. Formal Ontology, Conceptual Analysis and Knowledge Representation. *International Journal of Human-Computer Studies*, 43(5-6):907-928.

[9]   IBM Almaden Services Research. 2006. "SSME: What are services?" Referenced from the following Web site: http://almaden.ibm.com/ssme.

[10]   Katzan, H. 2008a. Event Differentiation in Service Science. *Journal of Business and Economics Research*, 6(5): 141-152.

[11]   Katzan, H. 2008b. Principles of Service Systems: An Ontological Approach, *Journal of Service Science*, 2(2): 35-52.

[12]   Kuhn, T. 1996. *The Structure of Scientific Revolution* (3rd edition), Chicago: University of Chicago Press. [Secondary reference]

[13]   Maglio, P. and J. Zysman. 2007. Toward a Science of Service Systems. *Sofcon 2007.* Carnegie Mellon University, April 30, 2007, pp. 5-6.

[14] Newell, A., Perlis, A., and H.A. Simon. 1967. Computer Science. *Science*, 157: 1373-1374. [Secondary reference]

[15] Sampson, S. and C. Froehle. 2006. Foundations and Implications of a Proposed Unified Services Theory. *Productions and Operations Management*, 15(2): 329-343.

[16] Selznick, P. 1948. Foundations of the Theory of Organization. *American Sociological Review* 13: 25-35. [Published in *Classics of Organization Theory* (4th Edition – J. Shafritz and J. Ott, editors), New York: Harcourt Brace College Publishers, 1996.]

[17] Smith, A. 1776. *The Wealth of Nations,* published as "An Inquiry into the Nature and Causes of the Wealth of Nations" in London, England (1776).

[18] Sowa, J. 2000. *Knowledge Representation: Logical, Philosophical and Computational Foundations,* Brooks Cole Publishing.

[19] Spohrer, J., Anderson, L., Pass, N., Ager, T., and D. Gruhl. 2007a. Service Science. *Journal of Grid Computing* (Special Issue of Grid Economics and Business Models, August 2, 2007).

[20] Spohrer. J., Vargo, S., Caswell, N., and P. Maglio. 2007b. The Service System is the Basic Abstraction of Service Science. IBM Almaden Research Center, http://www.almaden.ibm.com/asr.

[21] Sutherland, J. 1975. *Systems: Analysis, Administration, and Architecture.* New York: Van Nostrand Reinhold Co.

[22] Wikipedia. 2009. Ontology, www.wikipedia.org/ontology.

***** End of Essay 6 *****

7

SERVICE DESIGN

BRIEF OVERVIEW OF SERVICE

A service is an interaction between entities that co-creates value, where the entities involved may be persons or nonpersons, such as government offices, educational institutions, and possibly some form of automation. (Katzan [9]) A service interaction is ordinarily construed to be a process consisting of several steps organized to achieve an identifiable purpose. In the recent view of things, all products are essentially services, so that service and service design assume expanded roles in the development of cultural artifacts. (Vargo [23]) Service design, on the other hand, is a process that specifically takes an abstract idea and turns it into a pragmatic reality.

The entities participating in a service have differing roles -- often referred to as the provider and the client. Ordinarily, the client experiences a need that the provider resolves, changing the end state of both participants. For example, a patient with a medical situation interacts with a physician for appropriate attention and, in a nominal instance, a differing but tangible value is created for both parties in the service. In a similar, but slightly different instance, a property owner contracts with a landscaping service for a maintenance operation. In this case, the physical service object is the responsibility of the client, but the salient details are the same.

There is, of course, more to service than a simple service operation. The service itself may consist of several steps and require auxiliary service. On the part of the client, the process may consist of the awareness of a need for attention, scheduling of the service event, and other logistical steps. On the part of the provider, the service, per se, may require supplementary support service, prior to and during the service interaction.

In the naive view of service, as just mentioned, the number of participants is relatively few, and the time span is relatively short, so that the total experience can be conceptualized as a single service event. In major service projects, such as a major and complicated medical procedure, the construction of a large building, or a military operation, where the number of interactions is high and the time span is longer, an organizing framework, called *service design*, is required. (Saco [18]) The essentials of service design is the subject of this paper. They are based on the tacit knowledge that when we design a service or a product, we, implicitly or explicitly, adhere to a well-defined set of steps or techniques for scoping the problem, analyzing the design parameters, generation of feasible solutions, and implementation of the selected option.

FUNDAMENTALS OF SERVICE DESIGN

It is important to recognize that there is a reasonable limit to what can be achieved through service design. How an architect arrives at the characteristics of a structure or a physician deals with patients is in some respect a matter of personality and style as manifested in the cultural environment. In fact, *ethnography* and holistic studies are often regarded as important components of service design. To apply design principles to a situation, it would seem that several elements should be present. First, a designed service should have a stated purpose that can be given to identification. A behavior pattern is not a service, even though many social phenomena consist of elements that may be repeatable and regarded as service. Here is an example.

> In a hypothetical activity, such as going to business on a regular basis, a person would ordinarily engage in several optional activities nominally regarded as service. For example, a person might walk to the bus stop, take a bus to the train station, take the train to the location of business, and walk to the office. In the process, that person might purchase a newspaper and subsequently buy a cup of special coffee to drink in the workplace. Under another circumstance, that same person might take a taxi to the office. Thus, the ordinary process of "going to work" is not a service, even though it involves multiple service components.

The various constituent services exist as discrete areas of functionality connected by independent access points. Even though they support the contention that "services are everywhere," the various facilities are not necessarily connected in any requisite manner. Second, the service components in any endeavor should possess a necessary and sufficient relationship and not exist as a disparate collection of services. It follows that a collection of service components intended to achieve a predetermined function, when executed, is regarded as a service system, analogous to a missile system or an educational system. Service design is primarily concerned with service systems. Formally, a service system is a collection of resources, economic entities, and services processes capable of engaging in and supporting one or more service events. Service processes may interact or be linked in a service value chain. This subject is covered in subsequent sections.

The Evolution of Service Design

Historically, the role of science has been to investigate natural and societal-developed phenomena, and the role of design (and engineering) has been to build artificial things. (Simon[20]) However, there is more to the art and science of service than the recognition that 80% of the gross domestic product of most developed countries is derived from service and that more than 90% of persons are engaged in service work, so that service science, service design, and service innovation are important subjects. Some of the most obvious examples of the proliferation of service are "service to the community" and "community service to the individual and family," often evidenced by government programs at various levels. This is the basis of service as we know it today. Consider, for example, the interdependency of residents and families in agricultural, mining, and textile communities. An instance of the collectivism of service would be in the case of an unfortunate burning of a family barn in an agricultural community in an earlier generation. The members of the group would get together and rebuild the barn, frequently as a single event in a single day. The men would build the barn through cooperative activity; the women would cook and talk; and the kids would play and get in the way. The value of the collective service to the affected family is obvious, but the value to the community, as a whole, is the tacit knowledge that it could happen to anyone. Natural disasters would necessarily be placed in this category.

As the fabric of communities evolved into towns and then cities, states, nations, and regions, a social structure evolved and the need for leadership emerged. Leaders, such as the mayor of a town, would commit to services, such as fire and police service, and the birth of service design essentially began to take place.

The Environment of Service Design

A service is a socially constructed temporal event that possesses a lifecycle comprised of design, development, analysis, and implementation, as with most technological innovations. A service universe is a collection of services under consideration at a given point in time by a person, group, organization, or even a society. A service universe is typically a set of services, organized in some fashion to achieve a discernible purpose. Since service design is an eclectic endeavor, it would necessarily be expected to reflect differing points of view. There are two fundamentally different points of view of service design: the global view and the local view. The global view refers to the notion of a system comprised of interacting and complementary services. One could consider the global view as an external service description, useful for determining how a collection of services functions in order to benefit various people, organizations, and business processes. The local view describes and delineates the steps in a distinct service process, emphasizing the service participants and the complementary roles they play in a service interaction. The provider role is regarded as a serving activity, and the client role is, likewise, regarded as a receiving activity. Moreover, the collaboration adapts to the win-win model of economic exchange, since value is co-created for both participants. The complementary form of activity is intended to distinguish it from a supplementary form in which participants operate as partners to perform a stated function. For example, a physician and a patient exhibit complementary roles in a service, whereas a scenario in which two masons work together to build a structure represents a supplementary form of behavior.

As introduced above, service systems are social constructs that commonly encompass other services and are components of a larger reality. An organizational structure of this particular genre could be regarded from either of two points of view: as an economy or as an adaptive social structure. As an economy, it is a system of relationships that govern the availability of scarce resources and operate under conditions of efficiency and effectiveness.

As an adaptive social structure, the efficacy of a service event depends upon the dynamic environment in which an organization operates. Accordingly, a service system is a cooperative dynamically changing formal system, with a porous boundary so that the environment in which it resides has a deterministic effect on its behavior. Development of a service design involves the mechanics of service systems and requires three things: an appropriate operational platform, a design theoretic formulation, and a collection of relevant tools and conventions that are introduced in subsequent sections.

Service Design and Operation Lifecycle

Service design is one of the few disciplines in which the basic principles and resultant theory apply to practically all service processes. In its most basic form, a service is a value producing interaction between a service provider and a service client, consisting of a process conceptualized as a layered set of activities. (Ferrario and Guardino [4], Katzan [10]) It is useful to conceptualize the layers according to the following global service system lifecycle:

Service commitment
Service production
Service availability
Service delivery
Service analysis
Service termination

Initially, we are going to be looking at a global view of service design, where the lifecycle pertains to a set of generic services supplied by an economic entity, such as a governing body, a business, an institution, or an individual acting in an executive capacity. Essentially, the global service lifecycle provides the operational context for service design.

Service commitment refers to the formal agreement to provide a class of services to a service audience by a principal or trustee with the proper administrative control over the service environment. The agreement to provide fire service by a municipality and the founding of a health clinic are common examples. Service commitment incorporates a process for identifying where, when, and how an organization can make service more valuable to their clients and to themselves. A service principle commits to content and not to process.

Service production pertains to service provisioning, infrastructure, availability, quality management, and back-office processing. The producer is the agent of the principal in a prototypical principal-agent scenario. The principal and agent may be the same economic entity or different economic entities depending upon the scope of the service domain. The manager of a chain of restaurants and the medical director of a clinic are examples. Service production is prototypically concerned with client retention and acquisition. The principle element in service production is maintenance of the service infrastructure, consisting of physical facilities, operational procedures, satisfaction of legal requirements, competent provider provisioning, and dependable auxiliary service provisioning. The act of establishing hours-of-operation, for example, is a simple task in the domain of service production.

Service availability relates to the time during which a service is available. Commitment does not necessarily imply availability, because of a variety of spatiotemporal events that invariably occur when implementing a service. The service principal is concerned with scheduling, and other operational considerations.

Service delivery is the class of actions usually regarded as the service and is the layer where the service client comes into the picture. The doctor/patient relationship is a good elementary example of this layer, but service design usually is associated with more complex processes such as a medical provisioning that consists of several steps. The service provider, who could have a dual role as producer, is an agent of the producer as the primary source of service revenue and the primary provider of service.

Service analysis refers to measurement activities and the determination of value propositions needed to sustain service operations. To some extent, all services consist of the application of resources, and the success of those services is dependent upon how efficiently and effectively those resources are applied in a normative manner to a specific problem domain. (Spohrer [21]) The service analysis is normally associated with reducing costs and customer satisfaction; it is an ongoing activity in service delivery. Where implicit agreements exist, service analysis involves responsiveness, timeliness, and completeness.

Service termination reflects the inevitable consequence of a dynamic and evolving economic environment where a total service operation has been completed or has to be retired, because of insufficient activity or realigned opportunities. The global lifecycle represents a provisioning perspective of service systems. The basic tenet of service provisioning is the following. The client or customer starts out with expectations, and a service producer or provider should start out by assessing what those expectations are. However, not all service processes are successful. From a service analysis viewpoint, the success of a service event is dependent upon how accurately the service participants assess their roles. In order for a service system to be viable, it must exist and persist. To exist, that service must satisfy the economic goals of provider, client, producer, customer, and trustee, where the economic goals are known as the value proposition of the service. To persist, a service must be ongoing and not evolve into an unsuccessful state through one of the following situations:

> The participants' value proposition changes.
> The customer decides to engage in "self service."
> The customer decides to change service providers.
> The customer decides to forgo service.

Thus, cumulative service decisions from within the customer domain essentially determine the persistence of a service commitment. The service design lifecycle supplies the context for a complex service process.

Service Terminology

Several items of terminology are needed to completely describe the service environment. *Tangible service* is a provider/client event that results in demonstrable values to the service participants. In retailing, it is the acquisition of a product including attendant activities that change the ownership attribute of the associated product. However, the value proposition for a product may be determined from the service it provides, rather than from the intrinsic value of its specific components. In pure service, such as a people and possession processing service, value is created through the work performed on behalf of the client by the provider and that service does not involve a product. With information service, the service's value is derived from the transfer of information from service provider to the client. An *intangible service* provides value for a service participant through its affective component. Certain products, such as premium automobiles, special jewelry, and elegant real estate, for example, are typically associated with a high-level of intangible service. The intangible value of a product may exceed its tangible value.

A *primary service* is the core service for which the provider and the client interact to produce demonstrable value. It may be a simple service event or a complex process. Examples are a dental appointment or a lawn care service. A secondary service is a service that does not exist separately as a primary service and plays a supportive role to a primary service. Common examples are the weigh in and blood pressure checks associated with a doctor's visit and the acceptance and delivery of garments at a dry cleaning establishment. Secondary service is sometimes called supplementary or referral service.

A *facilitating service* is disjoint from a primary or secondary service and enables a client to obtain utility from a tangible service. Usability service, commonly associated with automobiles and computers, is a common example of a facilitating service. Another common example of a facilitating service is the purchase of an event ticket. In this instance, the event – be it a visit to the theatre, sporting match, or an amusement park – is the tangible service and the ticket is the intangible service.

An *auxiliary service* is independent from a core service and may be experienced before or after the primary service. A blood test taken prior to a doctor's appointment and a medical referral are examples of auxiliary services.

Service Execution

In order for a service provider and a client to co-create a service event, there must be some degree of locality to the situation, in the sense that the client travels to the provider, the provider travels to the client, the client and provider execute the service event in a third-party location, or they communicate via some form of interactive device and its corresponding media. Location is basic to service provisioning. When the client travels to the provider site, the location is termed a *service factory* and the client or the service object remain in the service factory for the duration of the service transaction. A service factory can be organized as a job shop or an assembly line, topics that are covered later. When the service object is left in the provider's facilities, the location is known as a *service shop*. The provider may travel to client facilities, as in the cases of consulting or nursing home care. With information service, the provider may reside in a remote facility and provide access through a *service portal*.

A related consideration is the distinction between discrete service and continuous service. There are many edge cases. Insurance is commonly regarded as a continuous service, as is banking – except in the cases where the customer visits a bank branch. A hotel stay is a discrete service, as is a train ride or a medical procedure in a hospital. Automobile maintenance, and household service are also usually regarded as discrete services. In the latter cases, when a service event is over, it's over. A follow-on service is regarded as another service event.

The primary objective of a service event is referred to as the core service that has tangible value to the service participants. The core service is conventionally comprised of primary, secondary, and auxiliary services, as described earlier.

We are going to establish five categories with which the execution of a service event, per se, can be categorized:

Category	Alternative
Modality	discrete, continuous
Diversity	heterogeneous, homogeneous
Temporality	active, passive
Complexity	low complexity, high complexity
Duration	short, long

Modality denotes whether the texture of the service takes place as a single interaction (discrete), such as a doctor's visit that is over when it is over, or it takes place over an extended period of time (continuous), such as an insurance policy. Diversity refers to whether the service can be performed by a specific provider (heterogeneous), such as a particular attorney or accountant, or any one of a group of providers (homogeneous), such as a bank teller. Temporality specifies whether the service is one in which the provider and client actively participate (active), such as a dentist's visit, or one in which the service participants are not actively engaged (passive) until a triggering event occurs, such as an insurance policy or a municipality's fire service. Complexity refers to whether the service is completed in a few similar steps (low complexity), or many different steps (high complexity). A hospital procedure or a home remodeling would reflect a high complexity; an appointment at the eye doctor or a car detailer would exhibit low complexity. Duration, not to be confused with modality, refers to whether the service execution takes place in a few hours or less (short duration), or whether it takes place over a few days or longer (high duration). In medicine, a doctor's visit would have short duration, and a hospital stay would have long duration. In transportation, a ferry ride would have short duration, and a trans-Atlantic cruise would have long duration. Clearly, the collection of categories is generic and reflects the underlying difficulty in attempting to be specific with a ubiquitous social phenomenon, such as service.

Foundations of Service Design

The preceding sections would seem to be quite lengthy for a subject that most people think is pretty simple. All you do is get a good idea and just do it. Right? You make it or write it down so someone else can do it. You can design it on the back of a napkin in a restaurant. Of course, the real problems are not design but innovation and entrepreneurship. Wrong! Nothing can be farther from the truth. With services, the actual problems are determining what to do and then figuring out how to do it. With some stakeholders, the actual task is to determine what is the real problem.

It is necessary, therefore, to point out that there are three parts to service design. The first is to develop a context for the service and then delineate precisely what it is that needs to be designed. It is necessary to solve the right problem -- to make it exceedingly simple -- in the correct context, so you don't solve the wrong problem at the right time or the right problem at the wrong time. This is as much a cultural endeavor as it is a procedural problem. A service takes place -- it executes, so to speak -- in an environment of people and organizational entities that is unique. Something that works in IBM probably isn't going to work in Google. The same design thinking is required if you are designing a pure service or a service provided by a product.

The second part is determining how the designer team is going to work with the customer team to design the service. Clearly, designing a service system for a major organization is totally different than designing for a small local group. For a variety of typical reasons, there is a higher degree of specialization in large organizations and careful attention must be given to the makeup of both teams. There has been some research in this area, and it seems that professional diversity usually trumps specialized knowledge. (Page [16]) It is frequently the case that it is absolutely necessary for a design team to develop a strategy for working with the customer in order to design the service that is needed in the first place.

The last part is not so obvious. Some service design teams must be better at their craft than others, because some service design projects turn out to be more successful than others. Here are some relevant questions in this regard: What mindset do good service designers have that not-as-successful designers don't have? What do successful designers know in order to do their job better? What service design tools are needed? What knowledge and training is needed to be a proficient service designer and how is this information imparted to prospective service designers? The questions are answered in two major sections: design thinking and design methods.

DESIGN THINKING

Design thinking involves people and culture. This subject is distinct from design methods that encompass design models and processes. When a service design involves a person-to-person interaction, for example, the efficacy of that interaction involves more than the exchange of acts or symbols. The point-of-view of the participants is basic to how the service interaction is perceived as an important component of the total service experience. The client or customer's expectations and the service provider's branding essentially will determine if a highly predictable or a highly variable interaction should take place.

Fundamentals

Design thinking is a discipline that combines the designer's knowledge, sensitivity, and design perspective with technical feasibility and design methods to assist a client in resolving a perceived need so as to provide value for the client and the designer. (Brown [2]) Recall that the designer will be working with the client to design services and products that the client will put into place when dealing with its customers. The prevailing mindset is that the designer is given a project, does the work, and then simply hands it over to the client for use in a predetermined operational environment. (Morelli [13]) However, nothing can be farther from the truth. In the modern view of things, the designer team will be working with the client team using the prescribed design tools to collectively produce a process that is experientially sound from the client's perspective for use with its customers.

In the past, most designers interpreted their role as being complementary to business and organizational strategies. Through globalization, much of production is currently being outsourced, so that global companies have turned their attention to local contexts. Thus, competitive advantage is achieved through innovation at the local level, so that the customer is no longer a passive receiver, but rather an active participant in the service process.

Design thinking has turned the process of design completely on its head. Instead of expecting a designer to take an existing idea or product and then make it more useful and usable to a customer, modern design companies -- especially in the area of service -- are expecting designers to create ideas that are more appropriate to customer needs, and in the process, make the service experience an important component of the design goal. Collaboration and prototyping are key elements of the service design process, as well as a variety of conceptualization techniques.

Phases of Design Thinking

In the quest for client solutions, a design project should go through three phases: inspiration, ideation, and implementation. During the inspiration phase, the designers and their counterparts on the client side confer, looking for new ways of thinking about the problem, spending time with the eventual customer through observational research or various forms of content analysis. During the ideation phase, the design participants look for inspiration outside of the customer base for insights into how the project may be scoped into new directions and new forms. Ethnography is a key element of ideation, since the eventual outcome of the design will have to reside in context of people and their culture. During the implementation phase, designers use a combination of prototyping and testing, through customer participation, to get the service (or product) right, relying on feedback and tweaking to resolve issues that surface. "What goes around comes around." So, implementation frequently returns to inspiration for a new round of research and development.

The key question is, "What mode of operation should the service designer bring to the table?" In doing ideation, for example, how does the service designer think about a design problem? The answer is quite simple, but doing it is not. Here are the modes on thinking that the design community has in mind: empathy, integrative thinking, optimism, experimentalism, and collaboration. (Brown [2])

Successful service designers use *empathy*, which in this instance refers to looking at the design universe from different points of view. What are those points of view? In a design situation, they are the viewpoints of clients, customers, end users, and colleagues. (Brown, op cit.) For example, a certain auto maker was asked why its cars didn't have adjustable seats and cruise control. The answer: The seats are just where they should be, and a good driver doesn't need cruise control. Times have changed, of course, but the point has been made that a good designer's thinking should reflect different perspectives, and not only those of the designer.

Integrative thinking means that a productive attitude should go beyond analytical thinking and look for novel solutions, perhaps from other domains. Tim Brown, President of the design firm IDEO, gives the example of a design done for a client's debit card service that models the prevalent practice of putting loose change in a container, such as a bottle, at the end of the day. The client rounds up a transaction to the nearest dollar and puts the difference in a separate account to promote saving. (Brown, op cit.)

Optimism refers to the underlying thought that an innovative solution exists to every design problem; all the designer has to do is look for it. The key element is innovation of which there is always room for a new twist or turn. Most innovation is not of the light-bulb type, but rather, it is the tweaking of an existing design. Innovation is cultural in nature, where implementation can be a major component of the design.

"Sometimes, you have to play with it to get it right." Admittedly, experimenting with the design of a service process is a bit tricky, but form and aesthetics appeal to our emotions, promoting *experimentalism* as an aspect of design thinking.

Lastly, *collaboration*, is required as part of each of the three aspects of design thinking. Clearly, it starts with brainstorming and ideation, but is part of the iterative component of the design process. Collaboration helps to identify requirements and supports differing roles among participants. Service designers, client, and customers collaborate to achieve service differentiation and competitive advantage.

Service Design Attributes

Creation of a well-thought out customer experience through a combination of approaches, related by a common denominator of a perceived problem statement, that include holistic design, cross-disciplinary synthesis, a useful and usable delivery system, and an effective and efficient service process, is the result of the five principles of service design. (Stickdorn and Schneider [22])

User-centered – The objective of service, by definition, is to satisfy customer needs.

Co-creative – The focus of service design involves the considerations of the stakeholders who should cooperate in the process of service design. (There are two processes: the design process and the service process.)

Sequencing – Any service design, other than trivial service endeavors, should have a timeline reflecting the service design process, and the state of the participants at that point in time.

Evidencing – A well-designed service should have a foot-print of front stage and back stage processes (covered later). The value of both tangible and intangible services should be clearly evidenced, as part of the service design experience.

Holistic – Service, of any type, resides in a culture. In many instances, the service designer collaborates with the client in its culture to establish service for customers, who may have a unique culture. Thus, a good service designer should be culturally ambidextrous.

In the application of the five principles, we are going to focus on five stakeholders from the global service lifecycle. They are the client/customer, the service provider, the principal, and the designer, supporting the contention that service design is not a job description but a process.

SERVICE DESIGN ELEMENTS

Growth of the service economy is driven by service consumption, characterized by a marked rise in skill-intensive service. (Buera [3]) Although low-skill services share many characteristics with the high-skill variety, they are characterized by low startup costs and a do-it-yourself mentality from a service design point of view. In order for a service to engender the attention of a principal stakeholder, an educated, trained, or experienced set of service providers, and a service designer, the service universe should possess certain key characteristics.

Key Service Characteristics

In order to design a service, it is necessary to identify a service model that reflects the design objective. A service model is an idea or mental representation achieved by abstracting the common characteristics, giving the designer a design pattern from which to start. This gives the designer a strategic direction obtained by matching client needs with a conceptual view of customer requirements. Accordingly, service has been classified along several dimensions. (Katzan op cit.) Three dimensions are presented:

> Service process – The service should provide a reasonable level of provider judgment, customer customization, customer interaction, and labor intensity.

> Service nature – There should be a precise specification of whether the service is people processing, possession processing, or information processing.

> Service mode – It is important to recognize whether the service is continuous as with insurance and banking or whether it is discrete, as with complex medical provisioning, and the judiciary and the law.

The development of service characteristics is useful for understanding customer needs. It is important to note, however, that the characteristics are only very general guidelines. A bank account or insurance policy may exist for a short period of time, for example, and a surgical procedure would seem to go on forever with follow-on checkups and related tests.

Conceptual View of Service Design Tasks

It is convenient to conceptualize service design as being analogous to human memory. There is short term memory that lasts from a fraction of a second to several seconds – perhaps longer – to support immediate tasks. Long-term memory exists to achieve more complex results and provide for operational continuity. So, it is with service. Some interactions, between provider and client, are perfunctory and immediate. The awareness that a class of service is required and the acquisition of that service are perhaps low-level phenomena, easily arranged and easily forgotten. A lesser amount of information, as needed, is necessary for this phase. The execution of the requisite service is more sophisticated and more specialized, requiring a higher level of judgment, customization, and interaction between provider and client. Design tasks mirror service characteristics. Accordingly, a service process lifecycle is appropriate to our needs.

The service process lifecycle can be viewed as those activities that exist between service acquisition and service termination – from both structural and operational viewpoints. From the structural point-of-view, the set of layered activities incorporate the service commitment, service infrastructure, service availability, service delivery, and the eventual termination of a service, as delineated previously. From an operational point-of-view, the layered activities describe service events and incorporate those transactable actions that constitute the essence of service.

Based on these definitions, the lifecycle of a service process consists of a loosely defined set of steps intended to co-create value for complementary service participants. It is useful to conceptualize a generic lifecycle as consisting of the following steps:

Service acquisition
Service invocation
Service execution
Service termination

Service acquisition refers to the process of identifying a service provider with the requisite infrastructure, and its corollary, the process of attracting clients. *Service invocation* involves the scheduling and logistics part of the service process. *Service execution* entails the actual steps in the service process including supplementary services. *Service termination* incorporates referral, warranty, and archiving activities. The requisite infrastructure for sustaining the service process lifecycle is referred to as the service platform and is related to the activities of the producer, covered previously. The service process lifecycle can also be viewed as a set of layered events. We are going to supplement the service process lifecycle with an overview of service design tools useful for a successful design experience.

Since service design is by definition a creative process, one would expect a wide variety of approaches to the subject. (See *Service Design: Practical Access to an Evolving Field* by Stefan Moritz (KISD, 2005.) An amalgamated view of six tasks is presented here, and from then on, the designer is on his or her own to develop an individual approach. When collaborating with a client in this regard, there seems to be no "right or wrong." We are going to cover the following six subjects: service view, narrative, process diagram, service blueprinting, touchpoints, and interaction design.

Service View

The *service view* represents the problem statement with its process suggested by representative diagrams. Initially, the designer is faced with the possibility that the client does not really know what it wants and has not thought the situation through. Several techniques can be employed for needs research: brainstorming, crowdsourcing, customer shadowing, contextual interviews, fictitious customer profiles – known as *personas*, and customer sequencing through a nominal service process.

Narratives

A *narrative* is a verbal or written description of a hypothetical run-through of a service process from which the designer and client can establish component services, touchpoints – events wherein the client server and customer interact, and operational conditions that should be met – sometimes known as *evidence* items. The idea behind evidence is to inform the customer what is being done and how well things are going. Here is a prototypical example.

A patient becomes aware he or she has a knee problem resulting from overuse, an accident, or another medical condition. After consulting with the family physician, an orthopedic specialist is recommended and a requisite appointment is made. The orthopedic surgeon takes X-rays and recommends a knee operation to which the patient agrees. A subsequent appointment is made for the surgery by the surgeon's staff and with the hospital for preop training. At training, the patient is advised of the steps involved in the surgical operation and is then given a complete physical examination, administered by the hospital staff in concert with an attending physician. The physical examination involves several steps. On the day of surgery, the patient checks into the hospital and is prepped for the ensuing surgery, which is a complex service event consisting of several steps. After surgery, the patient is attended by the nursing and physical therapy personnel following established procedures determined by the service participants for that type of service event. The patient undergoes prescribed independent physical therapy and has checkups with the surgeon on a follow-on basis.

From a design narrative, the collection of service components are identified that must be orchestrated in a real life scenario. The instances in which the patient interacts with the service providers are established – that is, touchpoints – and the various roles are determined. Methods for providing evidence that processes are progressing, as expected, are selected so that the customer's service experience is designed into the service process.

The design of a service is synthesized by a designer and a client, collaborating through information interchange, so that the design parameters are well-defined. As a service design nears completion, the narrative evolves into a service walkthrough, insuring the viability of the design from a customer's perspective.

Process Design Model

Process design model reflects the interaction between service entities. Unlike product design, the components of a service are a combination of integrated processes, people, skills, and materials that must be planned in advance. (Goldstein [8]) One means of describing a service process is through the use of a "bubble" diagram, often used in investigation to unravel a complex sequence of events. The degree of interaction between service components is clearly evident from a process diagram but the precise nature of each interaction is not specified. An interaction design is needed for that. In the referenced diagram, the service process from the customer's and service provider's viewpoints consists of the following steps. (1) The vehicle owner (*customer*) makes an appointment for service with the appointment scheduler (the *demand* manager). (2) The customer brings the vehicle (*service object*) to the dealership for service, covered by a service level agreement. (3) The customer interacts with the service advisor (*service facilitator*) to exchange service particulars. (4) The customer waits for service or leaves the dealership's premises (the *service factory*). (5) The service arrangement is entered into a computer (the *service scheduler*) by the service facilitator. (6) The service technician (the *service provider*) subsequently picks up the service order and performs the required service, often interacting with the service facilitator for additional information. (7) The service technician registers the service completion with the service scheduler. (8) The service scheduler sends a request to the service administrator for billing. (9) The customer interacts with the service administrator for pickup and payment resolution, and the service event has been completed. The process service model consists of five relationships: governance, information, service, ownership, and the service-level agreement. This process model applies to people processing, possession processing, and information service.

Service Blueprinting

A *service blueprint* is a flow chart used to describe the design of a service process. It is a tool for delineating the steps through which the designer or customer will go; it operates at two levels:

> The manner in which the designer and client collaborate to establish the design objective
> The steps that the customer will be engaged in to receive the service under consideration

We are going to focus on the second category, because it has attracted the most attention in the service design community. There are several uses of the design blueprint, the most common of which is to identify the constituent service events that are visible to the customer, such as the process flow, the provider interactions, and service bottlenecks. In so doing, five parts of a service process are identified: (Bitner [1], Zeithaml [24], Norman [15])

Physical evidence
Customer actions
Front-stage service provider actions
Back-stage provider actions
Support processes

This layered approach gives the opportunity to establish three lines of separation: line of interaction, line of visibility, and the line of internal interaction.

In designing, there are usually three main things the designer has to think about: what the customer does and experiences, what the service provider does in conjunction with the customer to gather information and execute service events, and what goes on behind the scenes to support the service provider. A *service blueprint* is a description of a service, and without that description, success will be a never-ending process of trial and error. *It is important to recognize that the customer and the service provider both go through a series of steps and the blueprint shows where they interact.* The behind-the-scenes activity has a flow also – usually – but it operates like a job shop on a demand basis.

The category of *physical evidence* is a catchall for the supplementary activities usually performed by the customer; they are necessary for getting a service going and sustaining the service. This is the acquisition phase and part of the invocation phase, mentioned previously. Prototypical examples are making a reservation or appointment, driving to the service facility, finding a parking spot, and so forth. It is important to include "physical evidence "in a blueprint, because it identifies activities that could be assisted by the service provider to enhance the service experience, shuttle service or valet parking.

The category of *customer actions* refers to what the customer does upon entering the service factory, shop, or information portal, and those activities performed during the service process, as well. They might include finding a table and reading the menu in a restaurant, for example, or checking in and going to one's room during a hotel stay or buying a ticket and going to one's seat in a form of public transportation.

The *front stage* refers to the actions performed by the service provider that are seen by the customer, either physically or logically, such as taking an order, selling a ticket, or ignoring a customer. The customer actions and the *front-stage service provider actions* are like two sequences, running in parallel, with a hypothetical dividing line between them known as the *line of interaction*.

The category of *back stage provider actions* denotes service activities performed by the service facility on behalf of a customer but not ordinarily seen by the customer. During a hotel check-in, it is the computer operations behind the counter that supply assistance to the employee in assigning a room and providing supplementary services that are expected but not requested by the hotel guest. In a restaurant, it is food preparation by the kitchen staff. The separation between the front stage and the back stage is known as the *line of visibility*. More specifically, of course, it is the separation between the front-stage provider actions and the back-stage provider actions.

Practically, all forms of service require support activities, such as the reservations computer in the hotel business and the infrastructure, operational and supplier functions in a restaurant. This form of service is known as *support processes* that are separated from the back-stage functions by a *line of internal interaction*. A blueprint of a service process is sometimes referred to as a story board.
(Stickdorn and Schneider [22])

Touchpoints

A *touchpoint* is a contact point between the service provider and a customer; it is sometimes known as a "service interface." Usually, the purpose of a touchpoint is to exchange information, and clearly, that can take several forms, the most prominent of which are person-to-person and person-to-technology, often regarded in the latter case as a computer and regarded as "self service." Touchpoint can be conceptualized as two processes, the customer process and the service provider process, running in parallel and exchanging information on a needs basis. Two associated metrics are of interest: the intensity and the duration.

Intensity is the number of touchpoints in a service process. *Duration* is the length of the various touchpoints measured on a time basis. Although the actual number of touchpoints in a particular service process and the length of time of each touchpoint are admittedly nebulous, the notion is positively correlated with a rewarding customer experience. When a patient visits a medical facility, for example, and gets only five minutes with the actual physician, the total service experience probably is not going to be regarded in a positive light. On the other hand, if the same patient were to see the physician several times during a similar visit, with some time allotted for additional patient needs, then the patient would regard the service experience as positive.

The notion of a touchpoint is basic to the concept of service. In fact, some service designers regard service as a sequence of interactions between the customer and service provider, such that the subject of interaction design is essential to service design.

Interaction Design

Interaction design involves the dialog between a person and a production or service, based on a series of touchpoints supporting the instantiation of a service. (Stickdorn and Schneider [22], Kolko [11]) The idea behind interaction design is to assist in making useful products and services usable. (Norman [15]) *Utility* (i.e., the notion of usefulness) is concerned with functional benefits of a service object, while *usability* involves an assessment of how well the interaction components are sequenced and how adjacent elements are interrelated. Interaction design shapes the behavior of the user of a product or service. (Kolko op cit.)

The design of a series of interactions effectively creates a user experience that determines whether the experience is successful or not. "The user experience is the totality of end users' perception as they interact with a product or service." (Kuniavsky [12], p.14) The perceptions include effectiveness, efficiency, and affective satisfaction. Collectively, the three aspects of perception contribute to the nebulous concept of service quality.

An interaction is a bridge between the front stage and the back stage that normally assumes either of the following forms: (Glushko, and Tabas [7])

Person-to-person services
Technology-enhanced person-to-person services
Self service
Multichannel services

Person-to-person service refers to a face-to-face encounter that provides tangible evidence that a service is being delivered. (Glushko [6]) *Technology-enhanced person-to-person service* refers to the case wherein the provider or the customer uses technology in creating an information-intensive service encounter. (Fitzsimmons [5]) *Self service* uses technology for enhancing the service provider's viewpoint in supplying service – as in self-service hotel or baggage check-in or online purchasing. *Multichannel service* refers to the case where a service provider supplies online and in-store services, as in well-known instances of book and apparel marketing.

CONCLUSION

It is difficult to draw a conclusion to service design, since it is a continuously evolving human-centered collection of diverse and creative activities aimed at an ever-changing goal. Service design is both art and science. Service design is innovative and global. Service design is personal and collaborative. But most of all, the discipline of service design is rewarding and satisfying. (Moritz [14])

We are experiencing a service revolution. The service economy is booming. Pure service companies are emerging, and product companies are becoming "solution" companies, as complementary services accompany products. Why is this the case? The product market has been commoditized, and as a result, enhanced services are used to secure a competitive advantage. Technology enables service, so that the relationship between providers and clients has changed. Technology offers choices for delivering service to more fully satisfy human needs.

Heretofore, agriculture, manufacturing, and service were regarded as the major sectors of the modern economy. Through service design, a new peer has been added: the transformation of data and information into useful knowledge.

SERVICE DESIGN REFERENCES

[1]   Bitner, M., Ostrom, A., and F. Morgan. 2007. Service Blueprinting: A Practical Technique for Service Innovation. *Center for Service Leadership, Arizona State University.*

[2]   Brown, T. 2008. Design Thinking. *Harvard Business Review,* (June 2008), p. 1-10.

[3]   Buera, F. and J. Kaboski. 2009. The Rise of the Service Economy. (www.nd.edu/~jkaboski/service.pdf).

[4]   Ferrario, R. and N. Guardino. 2008. Towards an Ontological Foundation for Services Science. *Proceedings of the Future Internet Symposium*, Vienna, Austria, 28-30 September 2008.

[5]   Fitzsimmons, J.A. and M.J. Fitzsimmons. 2006. *Service Management: Operations, Strategy, Information Technology* (5th Edition), New York: McGraw-Hill Irwin.

[6]   Glushko, R. 2010. Seven Contexts for Service System Design. (ischool.berkekey.edu/glushko)

[7]   Glushko, R. and L. Tabas. 2010. Designing Services by Bridging the "Front Stage" and "Back Stage." (ischool.berkekey.edu/glushko)

[8]   Goldstein, S., Johnston, R., Duffy, J., and J. Rao. 2002. The service concept: the missing link in service design research? *Journal of Operations Management* 20:121-13.

[9]   Katzan, H. 2011. Essentials of Service Design, *Journal of Service Science,* 4(2): 43-60.

[10]   Katzan, H. 2010. Principles of Service Systems: An Ontological Approach. *Journal of Service Science,* 2(2): 35-52.

[11]   Kolko, J. 2011. *Thoughts on Interaction Design.* New York: Elsevier.

[12]   Kuniavsky, M. 2010. *Smart Things: Ubiquitous Computing User Experience Design.* New York: Elsevier/Morgan Kaufmann.

[13]   Morelli, N. 2007. Social Innovation and New Industrial Contexts: Can Designers "Industrialize" Socially Responsible Solutions? *Design Issues,* 23(4): 3-21.

[14]   Moritz, S. 2005. *Service Design: Practical Access to an Evolving Field.* KISD (Germany).

[15]   Norman, D. 2011. *Living with Complexity.* Cambridge, MA: The MIT Press.

[16]   Page, S. 2007. *The Difference: How the Power of Diversity Creates Better Groups, Firms, Schools, and Societies.* Princeton: Princeton University Press.

[17]   Ricketts, J. 2008. *Reaching the Goal: How Managers Improve a Service Business Using Goldratt's Theory of Constraints.* Upper Saddle River, NJ: IBM Press/Pearson PLC.

[18] Saco, R. and A. Goncalves. 2008. Service Design: An Appraisal. *Design Management,* 19(1):10-19.

[19] Shostack, G. 1984. Designing Services that Deliver. *Harvard Business Review,* 62(1): 133-139.

[20] Simon, H. 1996. *The Sciences of the Artificial.* Cambridge, MA: The MIT Press.

[21] Spohrer, J., Maglio, P., Bailey, J., and D. Gruhl. 2007. Steps Toward a Science of Service Systems. *Computer,* 40: 71-77.

[22] Stickdorn, M. and J. Schneider. 2010. *This is Design Thinking.* Amsterdam: BIS Publishers.

[23] Vargo, S. and M. Akaka. 2009. Service-Dominant Logic as a Foundation for Service Science. *Service Science,* 1(1): 32-41.

[24] Zeithaml, V. and M. Bitner. 2000. *Services Marketing: Integrating Customer Focus Across the Firm* (2e). New York: Irwin McGraw Hill.

***** End of Essay 7 *****

8

SERVICE

A *service* is an interaction between two entities that co-create value, as long as the constituent roles are complementary. The receiver of the service may be a distinct service object. A service is a process resulting in tangible value when the associated sequence of steps is instantiated. (Katzan [9]) The term "service" is an overloaded word. The constituent steps of a service process may be service components arranged in a hierarchical or possibly a recursive fashion. All products are essentially services – a statement that must dismay economists and accountants – and some products and services may have an intangible value that exceeds their tangible value. For example, if a person drives a Porsche Panamera to his or her place of business, there is considerably more to the automobile product than the element of transportation. Once we recognize intangible service, it opens the door for an enhanced role for service in the domain of everyday life.

One's persona is a service signaling education, position, and leisure or social status. Form of dress, table manners, quality of speech, and even patterns of activity can also be construed as services. In fact, one's occupation can be viewed as a service indicating the social position of an individual. Are all actions and conditions a form of service? Probably.

Clearly, the scope of service innovation is enormous, and this paper applies functional analysis to uncover a wide range of applicable phenomena. In many instances, it is not entirely clear exactly who the provider is and precisely clear who is the client. A prototypical example is the common photo of an experienced physician, a trainee doctor, and a patient with the caption, "who's the client and who's the service provider?"

INNOVATION

Innovation generally refers to the creation of new or improved products, services, or technologies that are recognized by individuals, groups, organizations, governments, or society in general. Innovation usually reflects positive change, by making products or services more efficient, effective, more useful, and more usable. The operant question is, "for whom?" The provisioning of multichannel access to government services, in some jurisdictions, for example, is usually regarded as an instance of innovation. The client, on the other hand, has to make an "up front" commitment to that form of activity, so who really benefits? The client has to go out of his or her way to benefit from the innovation, while the government employee is free to engage in other activity, not necessarily productive in nature. Another familiar example is the ending of a news segment by referring the viewer to the station's web site with the familiar phrase, "You can find more about this story on our web site at www.xyz.com." This is clearly innovation, but its value proposition for the client is questionable.

There is an ethical component to innovation. Is the innovation of online shopping to entice people into purchasing something they didn't need in the first place ethical? This is an interesting question when considering society's inability to resist temptation.

Innovation is synonymous with change, for which there is always a reason. However, an operational adjustment resulting from a societal, organizational or governmental change is not innovation. Innovation is a change in a service – yes, all products are services – that results in a positive change to the value proposition for the provider and for the client. (Vargo [21])

Most product and service innovation – to revert to the older conception of products and services for a moment – is effectively hidden to the general public and to the consumer and occurs at the science and technology level to increase reliability and functionality. Engineering and design usually supply the following:

Products that are more reliable to reduce warranty costs
Products that perform better

Products that provide functionality not previously available
Products that look better

On the other hand, there is another side to the coin. At the service level, we are looking for services that supply the following:

Services that are more useful
Services that are more usable
Services that provide a better user experience

The latter category concerns elements that are human centered and give rise to discipline sometimes known as "service innovation." If there were an innovation cycle, it would cycle through the following activities:

Improve the process
Improve the result/experience
Improve the economics (value proposition for provider and client)
Improve the number of customers
Return to the first entry

The sources of innovation are generally regarded as *manufacturing innovation* and *end-user innovation*. It is customarily achieved by formal research and development or by on-the-job modification of design, commonly regarded as "learning by doing." There is a bias toward the former and many forms of diffusion have been developed to support that bias. (Rogers [17])

The economist Joseph Schumpeter [19] associated innovation with "creative destruction," whereby previously created productive forces are periodically destroyed to make room for new ideas, resulting in instability of the business cycle. Layoffs of workers with obsolete skills and downsizing to free-up capital for creation are normally associated with intense periods of innovation.

DESIGN THINKING

Design thinking involves people and culture. When a service design involves a person-to-person interaction, for example, the efficacy of that interaction involves more than the exchange of acts or symbols. The point-of-view of the participants is basic to how the service interaction is perceived as an important component of the total service experience. The client's or customer's expectations will determine if a highly predictable or a highly variable interaction should take place. Design thinking is a discipline that combines the designer's knowledge, sensitivity, and design perspective with technical feasibility and design methods to assist a client in resolving a perceived need so as to provide value for the client and the designer. (Brown [3])

Creation of a well-thought out customer experience through a combination of approaches, related by a common denominator of a perceived problem statement, including holistic design, cross-disciplinary synthesis, a useful and usable delivery system, and an effective and efficient service process, is the result of five fundamental principles of good service design. (Stickdorn and Schneider [20])

> User-centered – The objective of service, by definition, is to satisfy customer needs.

> Co-creative – The focus of service design involves the considerations of the stakeholders who should cooperate in the process of service design. (There are two processes: the design process and the service process.)

> Sequencing – Any service design, other than trivial service endeavors, should have a timeline reflecting the service design process, and the state of the participants at that point in time.

> Evidencing – A well-designed service should have a foot-print of front stage and back stage processes (covered later). The value of both tangible and intangible services should be clearly evidenced, as part of the service design experience.

> Holistic – Service, of any type, resides in a culture. In many instances, the service designer collaborates with the client in its culture to establish service for customers, who may have a unique culture. Thus, a good service designer should be culturally ambidextrous.

In the application of the five principles, it is important to focus on four stakeholders from the service environment. They are the client/customer, the service provider, the principal, and the designer, supporting the contention that service design is not a job description but a process.

DESIGN METHODS

Since service design is a creative process, one would naturally expect a wide variety of approaches to the subject. Six "tools" of service design are presented here, and from then on, the designer is on his or her own to develop an individual approach. When collaborating with a client in this regard, there seems to be no "right or wrong." We are going to cover the following six subjects: service view, narrative, process diagram, service blueprinting, touchpoints, and interaction design.

The *service view* represents the problem statement. Initially, the designer is faced with the possibility that the client does not really know what it wants and has not thought the situation through. Several techniques can be employed for needs research: brainstorming, crowdsourcing, customer shadowing, contextual interviews, fictitious customer profiles – known as *personas*, and customer sequencing through a nominal service process.

A *narrative* is a verbal or written description of a hypothetical run-through of a service process from which the designer and client can establish component services, touchpoints, events wherein the client server and customer interact, and operational conditions that should be met, known as *evidence* items. The idea behind evidence is to inform the customer what is being done and how well things are going.

Process design model reflects the interaction between service entities. Unlike product design, the components of a service are a combination of integrated processes, people, skills, and materials that must be planned in advance. (Goldstein [8]) One means of describing a service process is through the use of a "bubble" diagram, often used in investigation to unravel a complex sequence of events. The degree of interaction between service components is clearly evident from a process diagram but the precise nature of each interaction is not specified.

A *service blueprint* is a flow chart used to describe the design of a service process. It is a tool for delineating the steps through which the designer or customer will go to establish the design objective.

There are several uses of the design blueprint, the most common of which is to identify the constituent service events that are visible to the customer, such as the process flow, the provider interactions, and service bottlenecks. In so doing, five parts of a service process are identified: physical evidence, customer actions, front-stage service provider actions, back-stage provider actions, and support processes. (Bitner [1], Shostack [18], Zeithaml [25], Norman [15]) In designing, there are usually three main things the designer has to think about: what the customer does and experiences, what the service provider does in conjunction with the customer to gather information and execute service events, and what goes on behind the scenes to support the service provider. *It is important to recognize that the customer and the service provider both go through a series of steps and the blueprint shows where they interact.*

The category of *physical evidence* is a catchall for the supplementary activities usually performed by the customer; they are necessary for getting a service going and sustaining the service. This is the acquisition phase and part of the invocation phase. Prototypical examples are making a reservation or appointment, driving to the service facility, finding a parking spot, and so forth.

The category of *customer actions* refers to what the customer does upon entering the service factory, shop, or information portal, and the activities performed during the service process, as well. They might include finding a table and reading the menu in a restaurant, for example, or checking in and going to one's room during a hotel stay or buying a ticket and going to one's seat in a form of public transportation.

The *front stage* refers to the actions performed by the service provider that are seen by the customer, either physically or logically, such as taking an order, selling a ticket, or ignoring a customer. The customer actions and the *front-stage service provider actions* are like two sequences, running in parallel, with a hypothetical dividing line between them known as the *line of interaction*.

The category of *back stage provider actions* denotes service activities performed by the service facility on behalf of a customer, but not ordinarily seen by the customer. During a hotel check-in, it is the computer operations behind the counter that supply assistance to the employee in assigning a room and providing supplementary services that are expected but not requested by the hotel guest. In a restaurant, it is food preparation by the kitchen staff. The separation between the front stage and the back stage is known as the *line of visibility*. More specifically, of course, it is the separation between the front-stage provider actions and the back-stage provider actions.

Practically, all forms of service require support activities, such as the reservations computer in the hotel business and the infrastructure, operational and supplier functions in a restaurant. This form of service is known as *support processes* that are separated from the back-stage functions by a *line of internal interaction*.

Interaction design involves the dialog between a person and a production or service, based on a series of touchpoints supporting the instantiation of a service. (Stickdorn and Schneider [20], Kolko [10]) The idea behind interaction design is to assist in making useful products and services usable. (Norman [15]) *Utility* (i.e., the notion of usefulness) is concerned with functional benefits of a service object, while *usability* involves an assessment of how well the interaction components are sequenced and how adjacent elements are interrelated. Interaction design shapes the behavior of the user of a product or service. (Kolko op cit.) The design of a series of interactions effectively creates a user experience that determines whether the experience is successful or not. "The user experience is the totality of end users' perception as they interact with a product or service." (Kuniavsky [11], p.14) The perceptions include effectiveness, efficiency, and affective satisfaction. Collectively, the three aspects of perception contribute to the nebulous concept of service quality. An interaction is a bridge between the front stage and the back stage that normally assumes either of the following forms: person-to-person services, technology-enhanced person-to-person services, self-service, and multichannel services(GlushkoandTabas[7]).

Person-to-person service refers to a face-to-face encounter that provides tangible evidence that a service is being delivered. (Glushko [6]) *Technology-enhanced person-to-person service* refers to the case wherein the provider or the customer uses technology in creating an information-intensive service encounter. *Self-service* uses technology for enhancing the service provider's viewpoint in supplying service – as in self-service hotel or baggage check-in or online purchasing. *Multichannel service* refers to the case where a service provider supplies online and in-store services, as in well-known instances of book and apparel marketing.

SERVICE INNOVATION

Service innovation is the introduction of new or significantly improved services. (OECD [16]) Innovative services can be stepwise improvements, termed incremental innovation, or be radical innovations that are disruptive to the market or industry. In the former case, the innovation may be incremental but new to the firm. (Mohapatra [12]) Innovation incorporates inventions and insight that generate economic and social value. (NII [14]) In general, the source of innovation can be internal to a firm or result from a variety of external sources, termed *open innovation*. (Chesbrough [4]) In general, service innovation benefits both the provider and the client.

Through service innovation, something changes in the service domain, and a useful model of those changes is reflected in the den Hertog model that includes four dimensions of service innovation: the service concept, the client interface, the service delivery system, and the technology options. (den Hertog [5])

The *service concept* includes the manner in which the service is delivered, the customer's service experience, the service result, and the value of the service to both the provider and the customer. The *client interface* is descriptive of the roles played by the provider and the client, and is a prime determinant of the client experience. The *service delivery system* describes the packaging, delivery, and the mode of delivery, whether it be person-to-person or technology enhanced. *Technology options* suggest the use of computer and information technology to support and encapsulate the support the delivery of services. Clearly, the den Hertog model is a general framework that suggests the myriad of points in the service design cycle that are sources of service innovation. In actual practice, most service innovations will incorporate a combination of the four dimensions. (Wiki [24])

Miles [13] covers a set of four service attributes, each of which is associated with a certain type of innovation, normally resulting from a problem in service design, service delivery, or client experience. The general categories are: (1) Features of services associated with service production; (2) Features of services associated with service product; (3) Features of services associated with services consumption; and (4) Features of services associated with services markets. We are going to concentrate on features (2) and (3) under the title of "experiential services."

EXPERIENTIAL SERVICES

Clearly, service innovation is achieved through service design and is the reason that service design was summarized in an earlier section. Each touchpoint presents an opportunity for service innovation. With experiential services, the customer experience can be viewed as a "customer journey," built up over a period of time. As such the journey will consist of multiple touchpoints and multiple components. This approach will emphasize the role of the customer in service design. (Voss [22])

"Experiential services are services where the focus is on the experience of the customer when interacting with the organization, rather than just the functional benefits following from products and services delivered." (Voss [23]) We are going to use the Walt Disney World experience cycle of Departure, Savoring, Anticipating, Arrival, and Experience as a conceptual model for this presentation. The corresponding areas for innovation are the physical environment, service employees, service delivery process, fellow customers, and back office support.

The *physical environment* is the setting in which the service is delivered and is concerned with navigation within a service facility. (Bitner [2]) The category of *service employees* refers to customer engagement and includes the behavior of employees as well as auxiliary services. The *service delivery process* refers to the actions required to present the expected service. The behavior of *fellow customers* is instrumental in experiential design and can result from crowded facilities and unruly people. On the other hand, socializing can make a service experience more enjoyable, so that the subject of fellow customers is a particularly sensitive item in service innovation. Lastly, *back office support* indirectly supports the customer experience, even though the back office may not directly interact with customers. Back office training is important in this regard.

SUMMARY

Service innovation is a general subject related to either or all of three areas of study: the service product, the service process, and the service organization. Service innovation is designed into the total service offering through the traditional design methodology, as along as it results from design thinking.

REFERENCES

[1]   Bitner, M., Ostrom, A., and F. Morgan. 2007. Service Blueprinting: A Practical Technique for Service Innovation. *Center for Service Leadership, Arizona State University.*

[2] Bitner, M. 1992. Servicescapes: The Impact of Physical Surroundings on Customers and Employees. *Journal of Marketing,* 56(2):57-71.

[3] Brown, T. 2008. Design Thinking. *Harvard Business Review,* (June 2008), p. 1-10.

[4] Chesbrough, H. 2003. *Open Innovation.* Cambridge, MA: Harvard Business School Press.

[5] den Hertog, P. 2000. Knowledge-intensive business services as co-producers of innovation. *International Journal of Management,* (http://www.centrim.bus.bton.ac.uk/research/Rise/theme_denhertog.pdf).

[6] Glushko, R. 2010. Seven Contexts for Service System Design. (ischool.berkekey.edu/glushko)

[7] Glushko, R. and L. Tabas. 2010. Designing Services by Bridging the "Front Stage" and "Back Stage." (ischool.berkekey.edu/glushko)

[8] Goldstein, S., Johnston, R., Duffy, J., and J. Rao. 2002. The service concept: the missing link in service design research? *Journal of Operations Management* 20:121-13.

[9] Katzan, H. 2015. Design for Service Innovation, *Journal of Service Science,* 8(1): 1-6.

[10] Kolko, J. 2011. *Thoughts on Interaction Design.* New York: Elsevier.

[11] Kuniavsky, M. 2010. *Smart Things: Ubiquitous Computing User Experience Design.* New York: Elsevier/Morgan Kaufmann.

[12] Mohapatra, S., Cheney, D., Shapira, P., Youtie, J., Lamos, E., and A. Bhaskarabhatia. 2006. *Product and Service Innovation,* NIST, SRI International, and Georgia Tech Program in Science, Technology, and Innovation Policy.

[13] Miles, I. 1993. Services in the New Industrial Economy. *Futures,* 25(6):653-672.

[14] NII. 2004. *Innovate America,* Council on Competitiveness, Washington, DC.

[15] Norman, D. 2011. *Living with Complexity.* Cambridge, MA: The MIT Press.

[16] OECD. 2006. *Innovation and Knowledge-intensive Service Activities,* https://www.oecd.org/document/56/0,3343, en_2649_34273_362743360_1_1_1_1,00.html.

[17] Rogers, E. 1962. *Diffusion of Innovation,* New York: The Free Press.

[18] Shostack, G. 1984. Designing Services that Deliver. *Harvard Business Review,* 62(1): 133-139.

[19] Shumpeter, J. 2008. *Capitalism, Socialism, and Democracy* (3e). New York: Harper Perrennial.

[20] Stickdorn, M. and J. Schneider. 2010. *This is Design Thinking.* Amsterdam: BIS Publishers.

[21] Vargo, S. and M. Akaka. 2009. Service-Dominant Logic as a Foundation for Service Science. *Service Science,* 1(1): 32-41.

[22] Voss, C., Tsikriktsis, N., and M Frohlich. 2002, Case research in operations management. *International Journal of Operations & Production Management,* 22(2):195-219.

[23] Voss, C. and L. Zomerdijk. 2007. Innovation in Experiential Services – An Empirical View. Published in *Innovation in Services,* DTI Occasional Paper No. 9, (http://www.dti.gov.uk/innovation/technology).

[24] Wiki. 2010. *Service Innovation.* (hip://en.wikipodia.org/wiki / Service_Innovation.

[25] Zeithaml, V. and M. Bitner. 2000. *Services Marketing: Integrating Customer Focus Across the Firm* (2e). New York: Irwin McGraw Hill.

***** End of Essay 8 *****

9

COMPLEX ADAPTIVE SERVICE SYSTEMS

Social Constructionism

Reality constructed through social mechanisms is a dynamic process reproduced and maintained by social interactions. When persons or organizations interact, as in the execution of a service event, their shared perceptions of reality are reinforced as part of an objective reality [1]. This perception of reality is the basis of the theory of knowledge known as *Social Constructionism*, also known as Social Constructivism, wherein a belief is derived from the social and material setting in which it is produced [2]. In social constructionism, knowledge is socially constructed in contrast to materialism in which knowledge is derived from physical entities.

In a service system, entities exchange the performance of beneficial action [3]. Accordingly, service systems are socially constructed forms of interaction wherein entities perform the aforementioned beneficial action through the combination of people, organizations, and technology that adapt to the changing level of information in the system. The fundamental entity in a service system is the service event that exists as a socially constructed form of knowledge.

Complex Systems Thinking

It is customary to regard a system with a large number of elements that interact with each other or their environment as being complex [4]. The building blocks of complex systems are agents, which are semi-autonomous units that seek to optimize their behavior by evolving over time. Operationally, agents are aware of their environment and the behavior of other agents, nearby or in the distance, by developing action rules that govern their behavior [ibid.].

Animal populations and human societies develop complex organizations, but the difference in the level of complexity between the two is enormous [5]. Evolution to some extent can be used to explain complexity in animal populations and is often used to rationalize the apparent organization of behavior that is commonly observed. A human society exhibits self-organization based on human intentions and the collective development of nations, markets, and differing cultures requiring the property of non-linearity, which is the notion that the organization and behavior of a system is more than the sum of its parts [ibid.].

The emergence of organization in human societies, characterized by cooperative work, was first studied by the early philosophers Plato and Aristotle who recognized that citizens need to develop different skills and professions. In early political philosophy, the emergence of organization required a centralized system of political power. In the present context of service systems, similar principles explain how a complex system adapts according to three key principles: emergent order, irreversible history, and an unpredictable future [4, op cit].

Characteristics of Complex Adaptive Systems

Complex adaptive systems are based on relationships, emergence, patterns, and iterations [6], as well as other key properties that constitute what is known as the "ontology of the subject domain." For example, the universe is comprised of interacting complex systems, such as weather systems, immune systems, social systems, service systems, and so forth, which are constantly adapting to each other and their environment.

A set of nine key properties of a complex adaptive system are used in this paper and are summarized as follows [ibid]:

> **Emergence.** This property refers to the emergence of patterns resulting from the interactions of agents on an unplanned and uncontrolled basis. Examples: ant colony, economy, human brain.

Co-Evolution. This refers to the property that a complex adaptive system exists in an environment and also *is* the environment. Accordingly, the system and the environment evolve together. Example: the economy.

Sub-Optimal. A complex adaptive system does not have to be optimal to survive; it needs only to be better than its competitors. Example: winning basketball team in a tournament.

Requisite Variety. The property that determines that the strength of a system is related to the variety of options in that system. Example: democracy. In this instance, we are concerned with the universe of behaviors that a given system can produce and the options for change that are available [7, 8].

Connectivity. Success of a complex adaptive system is dependant upon the options for an agent to interact with its environment.

Simple Rules. The behavior of an agent in a complex adaptive system should be based on simple rules, so that the efficacy of that agent is easily determined and the agent can function in an autonomous manner.

Self Organizing. There should be no hierarchy of command in a complex adaptive system so that it can be constantly reorganized and adapt to its environment.

Edge of Chaos. A complex adaptive system should exist at the edge of chaos, such that its behavior can exhibit maximum variety in the space between equilibrium and chaos.

Nestability. A complex adaptive system can be encapsulated as an agent in another complex system. Example: a food system in a town that is nested in that of a country.

Clearly, we have been down this path before with cybernetics, automata, and artificial intelligence. Agents operate in an autonomous manner according to simple rules, or patterns; the system exhibits emergence and is self-organizing. When a complex adaptive system reaches a state of being good enough, it trades effectiveness for efficiency [ibid].

In the context of service systems, the transition of a service from an effectiveness state to an efficiency state is equivalent to recognizing the distinction between core and context activities. "Any corporate activity that increases shareholder value is core. Anything that doesn't is context." [9, p. 46] The implication is obvious; outsource context activities.

Behavior of Complex Adaptive Systems

Complex adaptive systems can additionally be characterized by their behavior at two levels: at the agent level and at the system level [10, 11]. At the agent level, two characteristics prevail: simplicity and multiplicity. Thus, an agent is characterized by a multiplicity of simple things, meaning, of course, that there are multiple copies of similar entities, each of which follows relatively simple rules. Recall that an agent, by definition, is nothing more than a building block of a system. *The agent in a service system is the instance of a service event.* Consider a doctor/patient scenario. Normally, a physician attends to many patients and a patient consults more than one physician. A practice emerges out of a collection of medical service events of this type. There is a boundary to the events because a physician specializes in certain things. There is also feedback because a patient returns for additional consultation. The practice is non-linear because a doctor gets better in providing treatment because he/she improves at diagnosis and treatment with an increased number of patients. There is, additionally, a relationship between nestability, the complexity of the service event, and the level of knowledge required. As diagnosis and treatment increase in complexity, an increased level of specialized knowledge is required to perform the event and the degree of multiplicity of events decreases. In fact, each service event becomes a mini-complex adaptive system, such that complex adaptive systems are nested within complex adaptive systems.

Next consider a service system consisting of a call/reservation center that has been outsourced for efficiency. An airline environment is envisioned here. A call-service representative services many travelers, and a traveler normally interacts with more than one airline. Again, the agent is the service event. A call center emerges out of a collection of service events, and a boundary exists because the call center is associated with only one airline. When problem situations arise, the service event is escalated to a specialist who applies an increased level of knowledge along with added functional capability.

At the system level, knowledge of the agent does not give a complete picture of the behavior of the system itself [12]. Again, two characteristics prevail: self organization and adaptability. As before, there is no hierarchy of control, and this characteristic is included only for completeness. Adaptability refers to the goal- seeking capability of a complex adaptive system where the end state is a measure of effectiveness.

Emergence

Emergence refers to "the arising of novel and coherent structures, patterns, and properties during the process of self-organization in complex systems." [13, 14] The manifestation of emergence is exhibited when a supervenient causality arises in a complex system than cannot otherwise be attributed to its component parts. Emergent behavior can result from a hierarchical organization (such as a bureaucracy) or from decentralized organization (such as an economy). In either case, the system behaves in a manner that is not predictable, and is viewed in some circles as the accumulation of side effects resulting from a collection of behaviors.

In the present context of service systems in which an agent is regarded as a service event, a handful of doctor/patient events or a few calls to an airline reservation center do not constitute a practice or a call center, respectively. What is required for emergent phenomena to occur is that the system has to achieve a threshold of simplicity, multiplicity, and connectivity.

Analysis

The original objective of this paper was to explore the conjecture that service services exhibit the properties of complex adaptive systems. The method is to apply the characteristics given previously to a representative set of service applications. Without question, the procedure is subjective; however, the discipline of service systems is a new science and a certain amount of subjectivity can be expected – at lease in the beginning.

The analysis centers around the potential for a given characteristic in a specific service application. To make things simple, a scale of low, medium, and high is used. For example, "What is the potential for emergence in an Outsource/Reservation application?" Table 1 gives a preliminary set of subjective results for three applications: doctor/patient, outsourced/reservation, and transformation IT services.

The results appear to be promising and certainly support the original conjecture that service systems are in fact complex adaptive systems.

Characteristic	Doctor/ Patient	Outsource/ Reservation	Transformational IT Services
Emergence	Medium	Low	High
Co-Evolution	High	Low	High
Sub-Optimal	High	Medium	Medium
Requisite Variety	High	Medium	Medium
Connectivity	High	High	High
Simple Rules	Low	High	Medium
Self Organizing	Medium	Low	Medium
Edge of Chaos	Medium	Low	High
Nestability	Medium	Low	High

Table 1. Subjective assessment of representative service applications using nominal characteristics of complex adaptive systems.

Summary

Because service systems are socially constructed forms of knowledge, the paper includes an introduction to social constructionism. An introduction to complex systems thinking was then given to set the stage for a survey of complex adaptive service systems. The characteristics and behavior of complex adaptive systems were then covered. Since emergence is perhaps the definitive characteristic of a complex adaptive system, the concept was covered in detail. Lastly, the analysis methodology was then applied to a representative set of service applications.

References

[1] Katzan, H., "Foundations of Complex Adaptive Service Systems," Decision Science National Conference, Phoenix, AZ, 2007.

[2] "Social Constructionism," www.wikipedia.org, 2007.

[3] Sporer, J. Maglio, P., Bailey, J. and D. Gruhl, "Steps Toward a Science of Service Systems," IBM Almaden Research Center, San Jose, CA, www.almaden.ibm.com/asr, 2007.

[4] Dooley, K., "A Nominal Definition of Complex Adaptive Systems," *The Chaos Network* 8(1):2-3, 1996.

[5] Mainzer, K., *Thinking in Complexity: The Complex Dynamics of Matter, Mind, and Mankind*, New York: Springer, 1997.

[6] Fryer, P., "A Brief Description of Complex Adaptive Systems and Complexity Theory," www.trojanmice.con, 2007.

[7] Ashby, W., *An Introduction to Cybernetics*, London: Chapman & Hall, Ltd, 1964.

[8] Wiener, N., *Cybernetics*, New York: John Wiley & Sons, 1948.

[9] Woods, D. and T. Mattern, *Enterprise SOA: Designing IT for Business Innovation*, Cambridge: O'Reilly, 2006.

[10] "About Complex Systems," Northwestern Institute on Complex Systems, Northwestern University, 2007.

[11] "Complex Systems," www.wikipedia.org, 2007.

[12] "Complex Adaptive Systems," www.wikipedia.org, 2007.

[13] "Emergence," www.wikipedia.org, 2007.

[14] Goldstein, J., "Emergence as a Construct: History and Issues" *Emergence: Complexity and Organization* 1:49-72. (Secondary reference)

****** End of Essay 9 *****

10

EVOLUTIONARY SERVICE DYNAMICS

INTRODUCTION

It is well established that service is a relationship between a provider and a client that captures value. (Spohrer 2007, Katzan 2008, Lusch 2008) It has also been recognized that service is a process, and that all products may in fact be services. (Vargo 2009) This perspective gives us a wide-open playing field for investigating the evolutionary dynamics of service provisioning in particular areas of concern. The purpose of this paper is to develop a model (i.e., a set of equations and relationships) that describes how service evolves through a metaphor of selection, survival of the fittest, replication, and mutation. We will be dealing with categories of service providers, because as Martin Nowak aptly puts it, "Evolutionary dynamics acts on populations. Neither genes, nor cells, nor individuals evolve; only populations evolve." (Nowak 2005) In fact, the model has implications for service provisioning within a service collective. (Katzan 2010b) A client selects a service provider within a particular category for a variety of reasons that pertain to the overall problem domain. As conditions change, the client may select another provider in the same category or switch to a provider in another category. In fact, the client may leave the service system altogether. This paper seeks to apply evolutionary dynamics to a population of service elements. In this instance, the service system responds to a population of clients that serves as the environment in a metaphor of service evolution.

Evolutionary Service Elements

You don't have service if you don't have clients, also known as customers or consumers, depending upon the context. Clients often have a choice among providers over a particular service domain. Some everyday examples will set the scene. In the medical area, for example, a patient could choose from the categories of *medical doctor, osteopathic physician,* or *chiropractor.* This might be regarded as a pure service, as would be the area of education composed of private school, public school, and tutoring. An example of the domain of "services that involve a product" could be a fast-food restaurant offering hamburgers, fish sandwiches, chicken sandwiches, and salads. A bakery providing bread, donuts, muffins, and cake would represent examples of a "product as a service," as would an automobile company. A familiar means of representing a set of categories is a frame of discernment, as in the following list:

Medical	=	{medical doctor, osteopathic physician, chiropractor}
Fast food	=	{hamburger, fish sandwich, chicken sandwich, salad}
Bakery	=	{bread, donut, muffin, bagel, cake}
Automobile	=	{sedan, coupe, convertible, van, suv}
Education	=	{public, private, tutor}

The key point is that the client has a free choice within in a service domain. Usually, the choice may change but not the domain. Thus, we have populations of service providers categorized by definitive attributes. We are going to study the evolution of the categories, as a biological scientist might study a species. Within a specific domain, members of a category have common attributes with enough variety to allow for evolutionary service elements, such as natural selection, replication, and mutation.

Elementary Operations

A client enters and leaves a *service system,* regarded as a collection of resources, economic entities, and supplementary services capable of engaging in and sustaining one or more service events. (Katzan 2010a) The client selects a service provider from among providers in a relevant service category that possesses sufficient requisite variety to enable that choice. (Ashby 1964) For example, a client may choose a particular physician from a medical-doctor category over a *medical* domain, a laptop computer over a *computer* domain, a kind of hamburger over a *fast food* domain, or a kind of vehicle over an *automobile* domain. We are concerned about the result of client behavior in such situations.

Within a broad service domain, such as fast food or medical treatment, the client has the choice of behaviors, such as the following:

Stay with that service category (perhaps comprised of diverse providers)
Change category
Leave the service system altogether

A service provider category encapsulates multiple services in the following manner: (1) A single provider performs multiple services; (2) A client can use a single provider for different service events; and (3) A client can move between providers in the category.

There is customarily movement by clients between service categories depending upon social and other metaphysical considerations, for which there is normally a cost and benefit accrued by changing categories. An organization, for example, may change consulting services or cloud service providers. Some categories within a service domain are more attractive for a variety of reasons, collectively identified as "fitness." When clients select a category of service, they are exercising the right to choose, known as *democratization*. Thus, the process of independent choice, otherwise known as selection, contributes to the fitness of a category with the underlying assumption that clients select the most attractive service provider, based on their temporal needs.

Service dynamics acts on populations of service providers within a particular service domain, so we will be viewing service through a service category lens. Service categories effectively "steal" from other categories by being more fit for selection and replication. The precise reasons that clients move between categories are not relevant to this form of analysis. The important thing is that they do it based on evolutionary considerations. In fact, even the client set is not important for this analysis, since, as mentioned, it serves as the environment for the provider set. We are solely interested in the kinematics of the behavior of populations of service providers.

Biological Metaphor

In this manner of analysis, there are two populations: a set of clients and a set of providers. A client selects from the available providers. We are not necessarily concerned with individual clients, except for the fact that they select a service category – of course, over a service domain with an associated frame of discernment.

We are going to refer to the collection of service providers in a service domain as a *population*, comprised of service categories, referred to as a *species*. Species evolve and attract more clients. Species also regress and lose clients. Evolution progresses through selection and replication. Regression can be viewed as the result of a lack of fitness.

Fitness is a complex phenomenon linked to the ability of a service category's ability to attract clients and evolve in a purposeful manner. An important component of fitness is a service metric, such as market share, sales volume, or revenue. This subject is covered in the next section.

Service categories further evolve through combination and division. New service categories can be formed by combining two or more constituent categories, sometimes known as merging. Service division is a process by which an established service category is divided to form competing categories or supply supplementary services.

As in biological processes, the essence of service dynamics is competition. Categories compete to enhance their values of the service metric and to sustain their position in the chain of categories in a service collective. (Katzan 2010b) As a focal point, one may regard provider behavior as reflecting "market share" and "sustainability."

Democratization And Monetization Of Services

In the marketplace of services, providers compete for market share, volume, or revenue, because there is a limited resource pool (scarcity) or a controlled growth in the availability of required resources. The selection process is a measure of fitness. The clients essentially vote for the provider that is most fit by selecting a specific service category, known as the *democratization of services*.

Once a service metric is selected, it is important to recognize a dependency on whether the population is fixed or variable. If the birth rate (b) and death rate (*d*) of clients is equal, i.e., ***b=d***, the methodology, related to fitness, is adjusted from that of a dynamic population, where ***b>d*** or ***b<d***. For example, if the purchaseability of a set of vehicle buyers is fixed, e.g., one vehicle per family, then a move from sedan to utility vehicle, for example, changes the service metric from the case where the client supplements a sedan with a utility vehicle.

Monetization of services refers to the "survival of the fittest" notion, such that a provider category can adjust its service provisioning in an attempt to change its market position. The form of modeling presented in this paper necessarily applies to both the democratization and monetization of service.

EVOLUTIONARY BEHAVIOR

Following Nowak (2006) and Olfati-Saber (2007), we seek to develop a formal description of client behavior as elements move between service providers over a frame of discernment. The provider network can be viewed as a complete graph G=(N, E), where the nodes (N) represent the case where a set of clients enlist the services of a particular set of service providers, and the edges (E) represent movement between the providers resulting from socioeconomic conditions.

Service Demographics

The methods of analysis are based on a collection P of *n* service provider groups over an area of endeavor A. The expectation is that a client will select a member of P for service. For example, a patient will choose among the distinct categories of medical doctors, osteopathic physicians, or chiropractors for treatment. Each category may incorporate one or more providers. Similarly, a customer of a bakery shop may choose a donut, muffin, or bagel – using the "all products are essentially services" (Vargo 2009) conjecture – where in fact there are several choices on the shelf.

Represent the categories of population P over domain A as the vector

$$C = [c_i], \ i=1, 2, \ldots, n$$

The proportion of the client population that selects a particular provider category is denoted by the vector

$$X = [x_i], i=1, 2, ..., n$$

where x_i represents the proportion of the client population associated with provider category c_i, where $\Sigma i\, x_I = 1$. The analyst may interpret the metric X in any manner pertaining to the analysis, such as the number of clients, total value of client interactions, or the volume of client service.

The attitudes and beliefs resulting from a prior service event or interactions with other clients affect the x_i. At this stage of the research, we are not going to consider client movement within a category.

Applying the biology metaphor, the collection of provider categories C are a species in the population P, and a category replicates in response to client requirements – or more accurately, client preferences.

An example of this form of replication would be innovation and competition based on increasing market opportunities. The notion of fitness applies here as the most-fit providers attract the most clients.

Service Kinematics

The status of a service system, under consideration at a given point in time, is therefore represented by the state vector:

$$X = [x_1, x_2, ..., x_n]$$

where each x_i reflects the proportion of clients that choose provider category c_i. Consider a reward matrix $A = [a_{ij}]$ that represents the reward that a client would obtain by switching from category c_j to category c_i. Thus, a service category replicates in response to client preferences. One could conceptualize a business switching for computer consulting services from one provider to another, but only if there is some measurable utility for doing so. When a provider c_i replicates, the value of its state value x_i increases based on a fitness measure determined by the values in the reward matrix.

Mutation

Mutation is an important element in replication based on fitness. The probability that clients in group c_i mutates to group c_j is given by matrix:

$$Q = [q_{ij}], \text{ where } 0 \le q_{ij} \le 1$$

Q is square row stochastic matrix of order $n \times n$ and $\Sigma_j^n q_{ij} = 1$. Thus, q_{ij} can be regarded as the rate of transference from x_i to x_j based on exogenous conditions.

SERVICE DYNAMICS

Several equations, adapted from mathematical biology, Nowak (op cit.) and Olfati-Saber (op cit.), are used to describe client behavior. In order to properly frame the problem of service dynamics, several considerations are useful for explaining the terminology adapted from evolutionary biology. As with most instances of socioeconomic behavior, some service providers dominate because there is a positive utility for their selection. The term commonly used to reflect a position is "fitness." The service providers that are most fit receive the attention, and not-so-fortunate providers adapt to better compete and increase their sustainability index. We are going to base the fitness metric on the reward matrix A, covered earlier. Mutation is also introduced, because even though clients are assumed to be rational, other considerations from the environment often apply.

Fitness

Fitness is a measure of an element c_i from category C based on the reward matrix A. The fitness vector is $F = [f_i]$, where i=1, 2, ..., n, and is computed as:

$$f_i = \Sigma_j a_{ij} x_j \quad [1]$$

and its average Σ for category C is computed as:

$$\Sigma = \Sigma_i x_i f_i \quad [2]$$

Clearly, the notion reflects the reward of switching from c_j to c_i.

The types c_i are competing for resources from the environment of clients, where, for example, one service category evolves faster, based on the reward matrix for clients and out-competes other service providers.

The basic measure of fitness is the degree to which a category attracts clients, represented by the column i of the matrix, resulting in equation [1].

Service Evolution

When $f_i > \Phi$, the state value x_i for c_i increases and when $f_i < \Phi$ the state value x_i for c_i decreases. The associated evolution value for x_i is computed from the following difference equation:

$$new\ x_i = x_i\ (1+(f_i - \Phi)) \quad [3]$$

where f_i is the fitness of c_i and x_i is the corresponding state value. The state value x_i is the proportion of clients that choose provider c_i. (Novak 2006, Olfati-Saber 2007) An example of service evolution is given in a succeeding section.

Example of Service Evolution

The example describes a service domain comprised of computer vendors, given by the frame of discernment C:

C = {Apple, Sony, Dell}

and the state vector X, as:

X = (0.5, 0.2, 0.3)

such that c_1 = Apple corresponds to a state value of x_1=0.5. A hypothetical reward matrix is given as:

$$A = \begin{pmatrix} 1 & 1.5 & 2 \\ 0.5 & 1 & 0.25 \\ 0.25 & 0.5 & 1 \end{pmatrix}$$

Each row represents the rewards of migrating to a category (i.e., the row) from the other categories (i.e., the column). Thus, a client would obtain a reward of 1.5 from Sony to Apple and of 2 from Dell to Apple, and so forth. Row one represents Apple, row two represents Sony, and row 3 represents Dell. The fitness vector $F = [f_i]$ is determined as

$F = (1.4, 0.35, 0.525)$

from equation [1], where Φ is computed as 0.82 from equation [2]. Accordingly, the new state vector, referred to as *new X*, is computed from equation [3], as

new X = (0.79, 0.106, 0.12)

reflecting an evolution to the succeeding state.

Mutation Matrix

A form of mutation, represented as conversion between states, is modeled as the rpw stochastic matrix $Q = [q_{ij}]$ such that $\Sigma_j q_{ij}=1$. The mutation matrix is computed from a weight matrix $W = [w_{ij}]$, where $w_{ij} = a_{ij}/(\Sigma_j a_{ij})$. A mutation parameter μ is defined, so that $q_{ij} = \mu\, w_{ij}$. (Olfai-Saber cp cit.)

Introducing mutation into the modeling, we can develop a more sophisticated replication model as

new $x_i = x_i \,(1+((\Sigma_j x_j f_j q_{ji})- \Phi x_i))$

Mutation is beyond the scope of this paper and presentation, but the notion of mutation is an intriguing topic for evolutionary modeling.

SUMMARY

The subject of evolutionary modeling based on the work of Nowak and

Olfati-Saber has been introduced, and its application to the evolutionary modeling of service provisioning has been presented. Equations for fitness and replication have been developed that differ from biological processes, but retain the requisite elements for a viable methodology. A relevant numerical example has been included.

REFERENCES

[1] Ashby, W. 1964. *An Introduction to Cybernetics*. London: Chapman and Hall.

[2] Katzan, H. 2012. Evolutionary Dynamics of Service Provisioning, *Journal of Service Science*, 5(1): 59-64.

[3] Katzan, H. 2010a. Service Analysis and Design. *International Applied Business Research Conference Proceedings*, Orlando, FL: IABR Conference, January 4-6, 2010.

[4] Katzan, H. 2010b. Service Collectivism, Collaborations, and Duality. *International Applied Business Research Conference Proceedings*, Orlando, FL: IABR Conference, January 4-6, 2010.

[5] Lusch, R., Vargo, S., and G. Wessels. 2008. Toward a conceptual foundation for service science: Contributions from service-dominant logic. *IBM Systems Journal*, 47(1): 5-14.

[6] Nowak, M. 2006. *Evolutionary Dynamics: Exploring the Equations of Life*. Cambridge, MA: The Belknap Press of Harvard University Press.

[7] Olfati-Saber, R. 2007. Evolutionary Dynamics of Behavior in Social Networks. *Proceedings of the 46ᵗʰ IEEE Conference on Decision and Control* (December 2007).

[8] Spohrer, J., Vargo, S., Caswell, N. and P. Maglio. 2007. The Service System is the Basic Abstraction of Service Science. *IBM Almaden Research Center*, http://www.almaden.ibm.com/asr.

[9] Vargo, S. and M. Akaka. 2009. Service-Dominant Logic as a Foundation for Service Science: Clarifications. *Service Science*, 1(1): 32-41.

***** End of Essay 10 *****

11

TANGIBLE AND INTANGIBLE SERVICES

INTRODUCTION

Shoppers patronize some brick-and-mortar stores to get a good price. Usually, it is for everyday essential items, and the service doesn't actually matter. In other instances, a bit of service is helpful, and the customer is willing to pay for a higher level of service. It is built into the price. In yet other cases, the purchasing process is paramount and approaches the product itself in terms of importance. Clearly, the product is a tangible phenomenon, and the feelings and emotions associated with the purchase thereof are intangible. In the former case, the assessment of the product is a left-brain function, and the affective considerations are right-brain functions. Each of the elements has a utility to the consumer, and the associated values are called the "tangible value" and the "intangible value," respectively. The ratio of the two is the k-Factor, given as follows:

k-Factor = (intangible service) / (tangible service)

The k-Factor would appear to apply to most, if not all, economic transactions.

This is a *working paper* on the k-Factor with the express purpose of extending the discipline of service science and providing a basis for further research.

BASIC CONCEPTS

The subject of *k*-Factor analysis is based on several concepts generally considered basic to service theory. The first is that some economists feel that all products are essentially services. The second is that a pure service event is usually supplemented by one or more support services. (A pure service event is a service not associated with a product.) The third is that many tangible services require facilitating services that persist for the lifetime of the core service. Lastly, some services, such as information services and some forms of possession processing services, are associated with certain attributes, such as convenience and accessibility, that serve as determinants of intangible services. This section summarizes the various concepts as they relate to *k*-Factor analysis.

Product as a Service

The basis of "product as a service" is the fact that most, if not all, products are purchased for one or more reasons that are reflected in the utility of that product. Often, factors of production, such as quality of assembly, modern design, and the selection of appropriate technology, determine the corresponding level of service. Table 1 lists several product attributes related to product service. The characteristics, given in the table, can be uncovered

Table 1. Attributes Related to Product Service

Overall quality of assembly
Good design
Modern technology
Use of appropriate technology
Avoidance of implementation determined by factors of production
Excellence of presentation
Availability of unique features
Reliability
Performance

through measurement, surveys, analysis, focus groups, and so forth. The notions apply to apparel, appliances, electronics, and automobiles – to name only a few instances. When a product is purchased for the service it renders, rather than the physical artifact per se, then the above attributes contribute to its value as a tangible service.

To sum up, a product is essentially a service in the sense that its tangible value is derived from the service it provides. A product also has an intangible value determined by product characteristics, price, and reputation of the manufacturer. In some cases, the intangible value of a product is greater than its tangible value.

Service as a Service

The tangible value of a pure service is determined by the training, experience, and infrastructure provided by the service provider. Supporting services – referred to here as *secondary services* – are frequently needed and the nature of those additional services contribute to the intangible value of the primary service. From a client perspective in a medical example, the utility of the service to the client determines the significance of the intangible service. In other words, if you are sick enough, how you are treated by the nurse does not matter all that much.

Information as a Service

The tangible value of information is determined by its completeness, accuracy, and relevance, as well as by a whole host of other well-known factors. The convenience of accessing the information and the reputation of the service provider are the intangible factors. In the case of "information as a service," information can be properly regarded as a product, and its usefulness is determined by the characteristics given above.

DEFINITIONS

A *service* is a provider/client relationship (Katzan [2008]) that captures value for both participants that can be individuals, organizations, or a complex arrangement of either one. Service operations are customarily grouped into three classes: people processing, possession processing, and information processing. Within each domain, it is therefore important to view the client/ provider relationship along the following dimensions:

Tangible vs. intangible
Primary vs. secondary
Facilitating vs. auxiliary

This approach focuses on the fact that a service event is a process consisting of primary and secondary services.

Tangible Service

A *tangible service* is a provider/client event that results in demonstrable values to the service participants. With an individual service participant, this is a left-brain function (LBF). In retailing, it is the acquisition of a product including attendant activities that change the ownership attribute of the associated product. However, the value proposition for a product may be determined from the service it provides, rather than from the intrinsic value of its specific components. In most people or possession processing services, value is created through the work performed on behalf of the client by the provider. With information services, the service's value is derived from the transfer of information from service provider to the client.

Intangible Service

An *intangible service* provides value for a service participant through the perspective of a right-brain function (RBF). Certain products, such as premium automobiles (Rosengarten and Stuermer [2006]), special jewelry, and elegant real estate, for example, are typically associated with a high-level of intangible services. As mentioned previously, the intangible value of a product may exceed its tangible value – both from a service perspective.

Primary Service

A *primary service* is the core service for which the provider and the client interact to produce demonstrable value. Simple examples are a dental appointment or a lawn care service.

Secondary Service

A *secondary service* is a service that does not exist separately as a primary service and that plays a supportive role to a primary service. Common examples are the weigh in and blood pressure checks associated with a doctor's visit and the acceptance and delivery of garments at a dry cleaning establishment.

Facilitating Service

A *facilitating service* is disjoint from a primary or secondary service and enables a client to obtain utility from a tangible service. Usability services, commonly associated with automobiles and computers are common examples of facilitating services. Another common example of a facilitating service is the purchase of an event ticket. In this instance, the event – be it to the theatre, sporting match, or an amusement park – is the tangible service and the ticket is the intangible service.

Auxiliary Service

An *auxiliary service* is independent from a core service and may be experienced before or after the primary service. A blood test taken prior to a doctor's appointment and a medical referral are examples of auxiliary services.

Discussion

In product retailing, product attributes determine the level of tangible service that is supplied by the use of that product. Obvious examples are design, technology, quality of assembly, technological invocation, and reliability. With pure services, the level of tangible service relates to training, reputation, dependability, and performance.

The level of intangible service is normally a function of the feelings that one derives from ownership of a premium product or the participation in a services event with a particular service provider. The demonstrability that one is successful, that "one has arrived," or that "one can't do any better" are paramount to intangible service levels.

Service Relationships

The service dimensions, mentioned above, namely tangible, intangible, primary, secondary, facilitating, and auxiliary, are associated through two concepts: coupling and cohesion. Both concepts describe the inter-relationship between dimensions.

Coupling is a measure of the interrelatedness of two services and reflects the degree to which changes in one service process require adjustment in the other. In a medical practice, for example, the coupling between a primary and an associated secondary service is high, whereas the coupling between primary and auxiliary services is low. Thus, a change in the primary service practice would necessitate changes to a secondary process. Interesting situations arise in analyses related to coupling. In automotive retailing, the three tangible service processes are the "sales" primary service, the "user service" secondary service, and the "maintenance service" auxiliary service. There is a tight coupling between sales and user service and a loose coupling between sales and maintenance service.

Cohesion is a measure of the strength of the relationship between two or more services – sometimes known as a measure of similarity. Thus, the service processes and participants share the same characteristics, when the cohesion is high, and are attributionally diverse, when the cohesion is low. The practice of two orthopedic surgeons would have a high cohesion, and the practices of an internist and a chiropractor would be low.

Service models exist for the types of services covered previously. Clearly, the roles of tangible and intangible services are relevant for product-as-a-service, service-as-a-service, and information-as-a-service

Table 2 gives a representative set of *k*-**Factor** values for several product/service categories.

Table 2. k-Factor Analysis

Product/Service	Primary Service	Secondary Service	Auxiliary Service
Premium automobile	$k \gg 1$	$k > 1$	$k \approx 1$
Luxury automobile	$0.75 < k < 1$	$0.75 < k < 1$	$0.5 < k < 1$
Volume automobile	$0 < k < 0.75$	$0 < k < 0.5$	$0 < k < 0.5$
Medical service			
– Physician	$k > 1$	$k \approx 1$	$0.5 < k < 1$
– Dentist	$0.5 < k < 1$	$0 < k < 0.5$	--
– Chiropractor	$0.5 < k < 0.75$	$k \approx 0.5$	--
Maintenance:			
– Yard	$0 < k < 0.5$	$0 < k < 0.25$	--
– Cleaning	$0 < k < 0.25$	$0 < k < 0.25$	--
Personal care:			
– Hair	$0 < k < 0.25$	--	--
– Fitness	$0 < k < 0.25$	--	--
Information:			
– Browser	$k \approx 1$	--	--
– Search engine	$k \gg 1$	--	--
– Portal	$k \approx 1$	--	--

SUMMARY

As noted in the abstract, this is a working paper intended to advance the science of services. Clearly, the k-Factor, as presented above, is a phenomenon that warrants further study. For example, consider the a-Factor defined as:

a-Factor = (expected service)/(actual service)

Is the k-Factor a predictor of the a-Factor? Another interesting question is whether there a relationship between the relative price of a product and the magnitude of its k-Factor.

REFERENCES

[1]   Katzan, H., Event Differentiation in Service Science, *Journal of Business & Economics Research*, Volume 6, Number 5` (2008), pp. 141-152.

[2]   Katzan, H., Foundations of Service Science: Concepts and Facilities, *Journal of Service Science*, Volume 1, Number 1 (2008), pp. 1-22.

[3]   Katzan, H., *The k-Factor in Service Analysis*. Charleston, SC: Southeast Decision Science Conference (2009).

[4]   Lusch, R., Vargo, S, and G. Wessels, Toward a conceptual foundation for service science: Contributions from service-dominant logic, *IBM Systems Journal*, Volume 47, Number 1 (2008), pp. 5-14.

[5]   Rosengarten, P. and C. Stuermer, *Premium Power: The Secret of Success of Mercedes-Benz, BMW, Porsche, and Audi*, New York: Palgrave Macmillan, 2006.

[6]   Spohrer, J., Vargo, S., Caswell, N. and P. Maglio (2007). *The Service System as the Basic Abstraction of Service Science*, IBM Research, Almaden Research Center, San Jose, CA, www.almaden.ibm.com.

***** End of Essay 11 *****

12

A DNA OF SERVICES

INTRODUCTION

In service science, a methodology is needed to distinguish one service from another and to define classes of services. A DNA of services is proposed consisting of a service DNA sequence of five letters corresponding to a five-dimensional quadrant-based scale. Each type of service is assigned a DNA sequence. If two services have the same DNA sequence, then they are in the same service class. The methodology provides a basis for classifying services, service models, and service systems.

SERVICE CLASSES

Service classes are commonly established in one of two ways. Using the hypothetico-deductive modality, we bring into play the notion of a concept and restrict our thinking to a certain area of awareness. We can view this process as one of looking at the world through a special lens so that we only see what we are interested in. Within this special world, we develop concepts that eventually lead to classes of service. Using the empirico-inductive modality, objects with common characteristics are grouped into a class and are represented by a concept. We can work backwards from object to concept because we are dealing with socially constructed phenomena.

Concepts

A *concept* is an abstract idea or mental representation that facilitates the recognition of and reference to objects in a specific area of interest. Concepts are important, because they allow us to omit the differences between things by abstracting their common characteristics. Thus, a concept is a mental phenomenon that allows us to identify and develop objects and processes in our world.

Service Classes and Events

Concepts lead to classes that lead to objects. A *class* is a material representation of a concept and an *object* is an instance of a class. Here is a *hypothetical* example from the personal services domain:

Service Universe: Services performed on a person
Service Concept: Medical provisioning
Service Class: Physician/patient
Service Event: Individual visit to the doctor

In this instance, the service model is "physician/patient" conceptualized as medical provisioning within the service universe "services performed on a person." Here is another *hypothetical* service model:

Service Universe: Services performed on a possession of a person or an organization
Service Concept: Custodial provisioning
Service Class: Office maintenance
Service Event: Daily off-hours cleaning of executive suite

The service model is "office maintenance" conceptualized as custodial provisioning within the service universe "services performed on a possession of a person or an organization." Even though the examples are not definitive, they demonstrate that service characteristics, such as those given, can be used to define classes of service models.

SERVICE DIMENSIONS

IBM Almaden Services Research (IBM [2]) and Fitzsimmons and Fitzsimmons (Fitzsimmons [1]) have identified five dimensions along which we can classify services:

I.   Service Process – using the degrees of Customer Interaction and Customization (by the provider) and Provider Judgment or Labor Intensity as metrics

II.   Service Nature – using the Service Object and Service Result as metrics

III.   Service Delivery – using Service Scheduling and Service Mode (continuous or discrete) as metrics

IV.   Service Availability – using Service Site and Service Execution (who travels) as metrics

V.   Service Demand – using Demand Fluctuation and Service Capacity as metrics

We can use the five dimensions as service model generators.

Service Process Dimension

Each dimension can be conceptualized as one view of a class of service models, and collectively, the five dimensions define a service universe. It is useful to think of the service universe as a point of view regarding the multiplicity of services that exist in a socially constructed world. The Service Process dimension is employed as an introductory example.

Here is how it works. Each dimension can be viewed as a matrix, such as the following for Service Process:

		Customer Interaction and Customization	
		Low	High
Provider Judgment and Labor Intensity	Low	Airline Hotel	Hospital Auto Repair
	High	Retail School	Doctor Lawyer

Each quadrant suggests a different service model, and the contents of that quadrant are examples of that type of service arrangement. Applied to a physician/patient service interaction, we have the following description along the service process dimension:

Service Process: Provider Judgment or Labor Intensity (high),
                     Client Interaction and Customization (high)

Clearly, this is a very good start to defining classes of service, but there are a few open items, such as the specification of the service object on which the service is performed. Accordingly, the Service Process is a necessary condition but not a sufficient condition for defining a service model.

Service Metrics

The service metrics deserve some consideration. The *Customer Interaction and Customization* metric refers to the degree of specific attention given by the provider to the client during the entire service event. When a client engages an airline seat or a hotel room, the facility is one of a select few possibilities and only a requisite amount of service is given to the client afterwards. With hospital service or auto repair, the service is unique to each client. The *Provider Judgment or Labor Intensity* metric can refer to three possibilities: (1) The amount of time the client receives attention when in the service process; and (2) The amount of time the provider is giving service when in the service process; and (3) The level of knowledge the provider brings to the service event. The service metrics are not precise in all cases; but it should be noted that our ultimate objective is to identify classes of service and not describe specific service events. (This comment will apply to the other service dimensions, as well.)

Service Nature, Delivery, Availability, Demand Dimensions

The other four dimensions are established in a similar manner. A summary description of the dimensions and the associated metrics are given in Table 1. Continuing with the physician/patient service interaction and applying the additional service dimensions, we come up with the following list:

Service Process: Provider Judgment or Labor Intensity (high),

Client Interaction and Customization (high)

Service Nature: Service Result (tangible),
Service Object (people)

Service Delivery: Service Scheduling (formal),
Service Mode (discrete)

Service Availability: Service Site (single site),
Service Execution (client travels)

Service Demand: Demand Fluctuation (narrow),
Service Capacity (not flexible)

The physician example is complete in the sense that we have created a conceptual view of a medical provisioning service along the five dimensions.

Service Considerations

It is important to recognize that a service model is not normative in any sense of the word. As an example, it doesn't tell you whether to go to a physician or a chiropractor. It doesn't tell you how to combine services or develop a service system. A service model defines one point in a five dimensional Cartesian space representing a class of services. What about service innovation? Simply go to a point in the space that is not represented and there is your innovation. There is of course much more to service innovation, but this is the basic idea.

THE DNA OF SERVICES

The previous section introduced the notion of a five dimensional Cartesian space used to represent services and establish service models. An appropriate name for this space is a *service hyperspace*, because that is what it is. In this section, we are going to introduce how the service hyperspace can be used to uniquely define classes of service. The DNA of services is used to delineate points in the service hyperspace. (In this instance, DNA is an acronym recursively defined as "DNA is Never Ambiguous.")

Characterization of the Service Matrices

It is useful to characterize the information inherent in a service matrix as a set of quadrants, as follows:

Column Metric

A	B
C	D

(Row Metric)

Super imposing the set of quadrants on the Service Process matrix, for example, is reflected in the following diagram:

Customer Interaction and Customization

	Low	High
Low	A	B
High	C	D

Provider Judgment and Labor Intensity

Quadrant A represents a *Low* value for the Customer Interaction and Customization (CIC) metric and a *Low* value for the Provider Judgment or Labor Intensity (PJL) metric. Similarly, quadrant D represents a *High* CIC value and a *High* PJL value, and so forth. The next step is to map the quadrants to a quadrant-based scale for representation in a service hyperspace.

Quadrant-Based Scale

Continuing with the Service Process example, a service with *High* CIC and *Low* PJL values is given a value of B on the following quadrant-based scale:

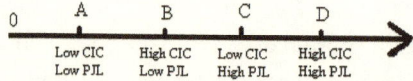

0	A	B	C	D
	Low CIC	High CIC	Low CIC	High CIC
	Low PJL	Low PJL	High PJL	High PJL

Table 1 gives the quadrant-based scales for the five dimensions in the service-quadrant hyperspace. Each dimension has a quadrant-based scale determined by the values for the associated metrics. Consider, for example, dimension #2: Service Nature. If the value for the Service Result metric is *Tangible* and the value for the Service Object metric is *Possession*, then the quadrant-based scale value for dimension #2 Service Nature is B.

Dimension #1: *Service Process*

Provider Judgment/Labor Intensity :: Customer Interaction/ Customization		Quadrant-Based Scale
Low	Low	A
Low	High	B
High	Low	C
High	High	D

Dimension #2: *Service Nature*

Service Result	Service Object	Quadrant-Based Scale
Tangible	People	A
Tangible	Possessions	B
Intangible	People	C
Intangible	Possessions	D

Dimension #3: *Service Delivery*

Service Mode	Service Scheduling	Quadrant-Based Scale
Continuous	Formal	A
Continuous	Informal	B
Discrete	Formal	C
Discrete	Informal	D

Dimension #4: *Service Availability*

Service Execution	Service Site	Quadrant-Based Scale
Client Travels	Single Site	A

Client Travels	Multiple Sites	B
Provider Travels	Single Site	C
Provider Travels	Multiple Sites	D

Dimension #5: *Service Demand*

Service Capacity	Demand Fluctuation	Quadrant-Based Scale
Flexible	Wide	A
Flexible	Narrow	B
Not Flexible	Wide	C
Not Flexible	Narrow	D

Table 1. Quadrant-Based Scales for the Five Dimensions in Service Hyperspace.

Here is where the service DNA sequence comes in. Each service model has a unique DNA sequence, based on the Quadrant-Based scale values for each of its dimensions. Moreover, the various dimensions have an order based on the dimension numbers given in Table 1.

Recall the physician example given earlier in the paper. From Table 1, dimension #1 (Service Process) has a DNA sequence value of D, because its value for the metric Provider Judgment or Labor Intensity is **High** and the value for the metric Client Interaction and Customization is also **High**. Similarly, dimension #2 (Service Nature) has a DNA sequence value of A, because its value for the metric Service Result is **Tangible** and the value for the metric Service Object is **People**. Using the same thinking, dimension #3 (Service Delivery) has a DNA sequence value of C; dimension #4 (Service Availability) has a DNA sequence value of A; and finally, dimension #5 (Service Demand) has a DNA sequence value of D. So the complete service DNA sequence for the physician model is DACAD.

Additional Example of Service DNA Sequence

The service that customarily known as "lawn mowing" is represented by the following script:

Service Process: Provider Judgment or Labor Intensity (high),
Client Interaction and Customization (low)
Service Nature: Service Result (tangible),
Service Object (possession)
Service Delivery: Service Scheduling (formal),
Service Mode (discrete)
Service Availability: Service Site (single site),
Service Execution (provider travels)
Service Demand: Demand Fluctuation (narrow),
Service Capacity (not flexible)

The key attributes of this kind of service is that the provider travels and performs the service on a possession of the client. The labor intensity is high but the service in normally not customized for each client. The activity is scheduled and takes a finite time. The demand doesn't vary and the provider usually has a limited capacity to perform the service. The service DNA sequence for this service model is CBCCD.

MODELS, CLASSES, AND OBJECTS

Each service model can be uniquely identified by a service DNA sequence. But, what if two models have the same DNA sequence? It could easily happen since many services have the same signature, as in the following examples:

Medical provisioning: doctor, dentist, chiropractor
Transportation: airline, bus
Home service: lawn mowing, gutter cleaning, window washing

If two service models have the same service DNA sequence, then they are in the same class, as defined previously. Recall, that the term "service model" is used in this chapter to represent a template for a class or an object – whatever is appropriate at the moment.

We can also construct a service DNA sequence representing a service class with no instances (i.e., objects). Because service systems are socially constructed forms of knowledge, we are not constrained by nature to describe only what exists. We can be innovative and design service systems to satisfy a variety of needs.

FUTURE RESEARCH

Service systems are assimilated from objects in a service universe. A methodology similar to the *DNA of services* is needed to formalize service systems in order to completely develop a science of services.

REFERENCES

[1]   Fitzsimmons, J.A. and M.J. Fitzsimmons, *Service Management: Operations, Strategy, Information Technology* (5th Edition), New York: McGraw-Hill Irwin, 2006.

[2]   IBM Almaden Services Research, *SSME: What are services?* http://almaden.ibm.com/ssme, 2006.

[3]   Katzan, H., *A View of Services Science*, Southeast Decision Science Institute, Savannah, GA, February 21-23, 2007.

[4]   Katzan, H., *A Client's View of Service Systems*, Decision Science Institute Mini Conference on Service Science, Carnegie Mellon University, Pittsburgh, PA, May 24-26, 2007.

[5]   Katzan, H., *A Client's View of the Quality of Service Systems*, Decision Science Institute Mini Conference on Service Science, Carnegie Mellon University, Pittsburgh, PA, May 24-26, 2007.

[6]   Katzan, H., *Service Event Classification: A DNA of Services,* Southeast Decision Science Institute Conference, Orlando, FL 2008.

[7]   Katzan, H., *A Reductionist Approach to Service Systems*, International Decision Science Institute, Phoenix, AZ, November 17-20, 2007.

[8]   Maglio, P.P. and J. Spohrer, *Fundamentals of Service Science*, IBM Almaden Research Center, San Jose, CA, 2007.

[9]   Martin, J. and J.J. Odell, *Object-Oriented Methods: A Foundation* (2nd Edition), Upper Saddle River, NJ: Prentice Hall PTR, 1998.

[10]   Sampson, S.E. and C.M. Froehle, "Foundations and Implications of a Proposed Unified Services Theory," *Production and Operations Management*, Vol. 15, No. 2 (Summer, 2006), pp. 329-343.

[11]   Spohrer, J., Maglio, P.P., Bailey, J., and D. Gruhl, *Steps Toward a Science of Service Systems,* IBM Research, Almaden Research Center, San Jose, CA, www.almaden.ibm.com/asr, 2007.

[12]   Sutherland, J.W., *Systems: Analysis, Administration, and Architecture,* New York: Van Nostrand Reinhold Co., 1975.

***** End of Essay 12 *****

13

SERVICE AND GOVERNMENT

SERVICE AND GOVERNMENT

Most persons in modern society require government and service to sustain a happy and prosperous life. Similarly, organizations need government and service to satisfy their requisite objectives. Through the economic concepts of specialization and division of labor, both entities, i.e., government and service, provide needed assets to their associated participants. [Smith 1776] Both notions are needed in order to sustain everyday activities and each has an upside and a downside. Government is expected to keep us safe and secure and provides the where withal to participate freely in our personal affairs. Similarly, service is used to extend personal achievement. The downside is obvious; we are essentially locked into societal norms and expectations, as providers and clients of services in whatever form they may take. Both phenomena are ingrained social concepts established by social interaction: luxury once experienced becomes a necessity, and similarly, wrongs that are not given proper attention are implicitly regarded as being right. Of course, there are differing views on the subject. Some persons when voting regard less as more – that is, less government is preferred. Others think that more government provides greater benefit for the most people. We are going to take the position that the idea of looking at government from a service perspective, however nebulous, has substantial value and is worth considering from an academic perspective; moreover, it would seem there is something inherently interesting in the subject matter.

Service Concepts

Most persons and organizations prefer to take advantage of service, since it is convenient and economical to engage a service in one of the modalities mentioned above. In its most general sense, *service* is regarded as a provider/client collaboration that creates and captures value for both participants. Both entities contribute in the interchange and both benefit, even though the sense of participation is diverse and varies between different forms of service execution. [Katzan 2008] A prototypical example is the relationship between a doctor and patient that relies on the participation of both persons, since both entities are required in order for the service to be instantiated. Moreover, a doctor's service varies between patients and yields different results, depending on the situation. This characteristic is typical of most service, such as auto repair and various forms of social service. The entity supplying the service is known as the *service provider* and the entity receiving the service is known as the *service client*. The domain of service providers includes individuals, teams, products, electronic systems, groups, and ad hoc units organized to execute a particular service delivery scenario. Similarly, service clients include persons, groups, social organizations, governments, and commercial entities. In some cases, the object receiving the service is the responsibility of the client, as in cleaning and repair services. In this instance, the entity receiving the service is known as the *service object*. Many forms of service delivered to objects under the jurisdiction of a service client exist in everyday life, as in automobile repair, child-care, and so forth. It is important to recognize that a particular instance of an actual service is created when it is instantiated – that is, when it is performed and not beforehand. Thus, a service is a process. It is possible to conceptualize a service domain as a universe in which providers and clients float around and connect to execute a service, and perhaps separate after the service event has been completed.

A particular service is often complex requiring supplementary and subsidiary services, so that a complex chain of services, called a *service system* is required to achieve a particular result. Thus a service system is analogous to a wide range of activities and artifacts, such as a missile system, an educational system, or a medical system. Many commercial activities, such as airline transportation, are based solely on service, and in other cases, service is only a part of a complicated commercial arrangement, such as vehicle retailing. Many business firms specialize in providing service. Industrial processes are outsourced to other companies and other countries. Service design is also a field of study in art and design curricula. Governmental and educational work is a service, and religious groups provide a service. Military personnel are designated as being in the service. The manufacturing process uses services to establish products that actually supply a service. Most social, commercial, educational, and governmental activities are actually service, even though the participants do not ordinarily regard their work as service. Perhaps, it doesn't really matter if a surgeon is performing surgery or service, but in the case of government, it does matter, because service is all there is.

Government

It is customary to view government in the context of the rule of law, the rights of the people, and the need for order, stability, and security. Academics as early as Plato recognized the advantage of having a foundation for government in social understanding, the interrelationship of human good and political good, and the justification for political power. In modern society, man cannot develop as a rational individual in the absence of a social organization and cannot physically survive without the assistance of additional human service. A political association is an outgrowth of human needs and therefore exists as a community of shared interests. It is the nature of the set of shared interests that gives a political organization its character and distinguishes it from a collection of people that happen to exist in the same place.

In primitive cultures, survivability was a key activity and cooperation between individuals was practically insured. Civilizations matured through a common cause and mutual collaboration garnered from a sense of duty and physical attachment. As society progressed, however, and grew in size, individuals relaxed in their duty and commitment to the common good. Thus, the establishment of a government was necessitated to manage defects in moral value. [Paine 1776] Clearly, this led to questions on how governments are organized, how they could be organized, and how they should be organized. [Aristotle, op cit.] Nevertheless, the primary reason for government continues to be economic efficiency and security.

BASIC SERVICE ELEMENTS

Most services are derived from societal needs, such as medical care, fire and personal safety, and educational assistance. Products are also derived from people's needs. The two differ because a service is a process that is derived from a specific need and is created at the point of instantiation, that is, when the service event actually occurs. Products are created, on the other hand, from anticipated needs and are created independently of the specific entities that will eventually use them. Accepting the fact that some products are assembled as special orders, the majority of products are manufactured beforehand and held until purchase. That said, products in themselves are essentially services, because the use of a product usually provides a service. [Norman 2011] A vehicle that entails transportation is a service. A famous painting, displayed in a suitable place, also provides a service to the owner, although its value is totally different; it supplies an intangible benefit to its owner. This section is intended to provide a bridge between service and government.

Tangible and Intangible Service

A *tangible service* is a provider/client event that results in demonstrable value to the service participants. In people or possession processing service, value is created through the work performed on behalf of the client by the provider. With information services, the value of the service is derived from the transfer of information from the provider entity to the client. The value proposition for a product is determined from the service it provides, rather then from the intrinsic value of its specific components. A tangible service is something that is observable in the real world and delivers results that are utilitarian and measurable.

An *intangible service* provides an affective value for a service participant through the feeling one obtains from a service interaction or the ownership of a product. Certain products, such as premium automobiles, special jewelry, and elegant real estate are typically associated with this category. The results from intangible service are affective and hedonistic. Often, the education or affiliation of a service provider supplies intangible value over and above tangible value.

Many forms of service incorporate both tangible and intangible components, such as a luxury residence or a special automobile.

Service Process and Organization

At the general level, an organizational entity that provides a service normally goes through a service lifecycle consisting of service commitment, service production, service availability, service delivery, service analysis, and service termination. As such, the service organization can be characterized, as being composed of a layered set of activities that constitute a value chain for a service, comprised of people, technology, and organizations. This is essentially a process view of generic services supplied by a governmental or economic entity, such as a governing body, a business, an institution, or an individual acting in a service capacity. *Service commitment* refers to the formal agreement to provide a class of services to a service audience by a principal or trustee with proper administrative control over the service domain. The agreement, such as a charter, to provide fire service by a municipality and the establishment of a health clinic are common examples. The mayor of a city is a common example of a service principal. *Service production* pertains to the operational aspects of service provisioning that encompass service design, infrastructure, availability, quality management, and back-office processing. The producer is the agent of the principal in a prototypical principal-agent scenario. The principal and the agent may be the same economic entity or different entities in a distinct service relationship. The producer is responsible for insuring that the resources are available to execute a service, including those persons charged with performing that service. *Service availability* denotes the time when a service is available, including initiation and termination dates and times. *Service delivery* is the comprehensive class of activities usually regarded as the "service" and is the layer where the service client comes into the picture. The service provider, who could have a dual role as a producer, is an agent of the producer as the primary source of service revenue and is the primary provider of service. Service delivery normally consists of several inherent services constituting a service value chain. *Service analysis* refers to the measurement activities and the determination of value propositions needed to sustain service operations. *Service termination* reflects the inevitable consequence of evolving services where a total service operation has to be retired, because of insufficient activity or realigned opportunities. [Katzan 2009] In government, many services are never retired, because of traditional budgeting procedures.

Service Knowledge

There is a body of knowledge, however, that supports the conjecture that a set of principles governs the operation of services, and that the knowledge contained therein has a basis in modern Philosophy. In social

221

constructivism, individuals and groups participate in a perceived reality, and create an element of knowledge, as espoused by the philosophical doctrine of Equal Validity. [Bognossian 2006] Equal Validity suggests the notion that other means of knowing exist in addition to the factual predominance of scientific investigation. As an example of constructivism, consider a simple wooden chair developed in antiquity. A chair is often made from wood that has been determined as useful to the purpose. Clearly, wood exists as a natural phenomenon, independently of its various uses. The precise form and substance of a chair, however, is a socially constructed form of knowledge that none but the hardened skeptic would deny is a valid form of knowledge. So it is with service. Service systems are socially constructed forms of interaction wherein entities exchange beneficial forms of action through the combination of people and technologies that adapt to the changing level of information in the system. Thus, service is a social reality constructed through a dynamic process replicated and maintained by social interactions within a service and between services. The notion of equal validity would apply to the perception of government, depending, of course, whether you are inside or outside of the agency's domain. If an individual is outside of a governmental agency, then that agency is providing a service to the citizen involved. If an employee is in the government, then that person is supplying a service to the agency – recognizing the duality of employment, as described in the next section.

Structural Dynamics of Service

A service process incorporates several well-known steps that constitute what is commonly regarded as the service: service acquisition, service invocation, service execution, and service termination. More will be said later about this service process lifecycle. Clearly, this is a provider view of service. The prevailing opinion is that the client is involved as a secondary participant. However, what would occur if there were no clients. Thus, a client provides a service to the provider by engaging in the service process as being a receiver of service. The concept is that there is a certain duality in services, wherein the client depends on the provider and the provider depends on the client. We will refer to this phenomenon as a *service duality*. The provider and the client, in the most general sense regarding service, are on equal footing.

In many instances, the provider and client are not singular but are groups. A group of service providers, known as a *provider set*, is a collection of service systems designed to support a particular endeavor in its respective domain, such as a university, medical group, or even a newspaper. Each element in the set provides a specific service to a client. Associated with the provider set is a *client set* composed of elements that function in a complementary manner with provider set elements to instantiate a service event. A service is thereby an interaction between an element from the provider set and an element from the client set, represented as a mapping between the sets. Accordingly, the collection of mappings is a *service set*. It follows that a *service collective* is a 3-tuple consisting of a provider set, a client set, and a service set, all of which can interact through an eclectic platform designed to sustain a unified service system. A unified service system is created when a client set is combined with the provider and service sets, and the inherent process is called *unification*.

Examples of service collectives are commonplace. A university, for example, provides services to students. The provider set would consist of administrative, student, and academic services. The students comprise the client set. Similarly, a newspaper consists of sections, such as sports news, national news, international news, financial news, and so forth. Readers are the clients. In both instances, not all clients use all of the services, and a section of providers does not supply all services.

A *service value chain* is a progression of activities adopted to materialize a service. Not all service resources perform functions that are specifically evident in a provider/client interaction. In fact, there are three major stages in a service value chain: service commitment, service production, and service delivery. The three stages are collectively referred to as service provisioning. When practitioners refer to service, they normally mean the service delivery stage.

In many cases, the provider set operates as a connected service system that interacts through shared information to provide a service. Two forms are clearly distinguished: flow and interactive. In a *flow system*, information is passed between service providers in a sequential basis. Operationally adjacent providers are coupled to provide service delivery. Essentially, one provider performs the initial step in a service procedure; a second provider performs a second step; and so forth. In an *interactive system*, members of a collection of providers interact on a needs basis to execute a service. Thus, the provider set can be viewed as a partitioned set in which sections demonstrate coupling or cohesion.

Duality and Collaboration

In the classic view of service, the roles of the provider and client are not symmetrical. In the most general sense, and even though the provider supplies a service to the client, and the client provides a service to the provider by being a client, the roles each entity plays are markedly different. In actuality, a team of providers may supply the service, and the client may be a singleton. For example, a team of doctors may service a single patient. The converse is also true, in the sense that a mayor provides leadership to an entire town. As mentioned earlier, the client provides a reciprocal service to the provider. This is an example of *service duality*. It is conceivable that service duality is a form of exchangeable value in service. [Katzan 2010]

In some instances, a set of service providers collaborates to execute a service. A *primary service* is the core service for which the provider and the client interact to produce demonstrable value. Accordingly, the key person, in a human instance, is the *primary service provider*, and in all but exceedingly simple cases, that person has helpers that provide secondary services. A *secondary service* is a service that ordinarily does not exist separately as a primary service and plays a supportive role to a core service. A doctor that supports a surgeon is functioning as a *secondary service provider. It is important to note, at this point, that the name "secondary service provider" does not imply capability, but what is actually performed during the execution of a service process.* The notion of a secondary service traditionally encompasses separate functions involved in the performance of the core service process, existing in close physical and temporal proximity. A core service is dependent upon a secondary service, and the reverse is also true. The cohesion between core and secondary service processes is high. When this phenomenon occurs, the core and secondary service providers are regarded as collaborating in the service process. Examples of secondary services are numerous and have a substantial variation. Three instances are the weigh in and blood pressure checks associated with a doctor's visit, the acceptance and delivery of garments at a dry cleaning establishment, and the routine support functions performed in support of an automobile mechanic.

When two service providers are cooperating to perform a task, or set of tasks, but working independently as with a couple of masons building a structure, the concept of core and secondary service processes does not necessarily apply, since the cohesion of the two participants is low.

There are two additional forms of supporting service: facilitating service and auxiliary service. A *facilitating service* is disjoint from a primary or secondary service and enables a client to obtain utility from a service, such as instruction on how to use an automobile or a computer. Another example is a ticket agency that provides access to a tangible event, such as the theatre or an amusement park. An *auxiliary service* is independent from a core service and takes place before or after the core service. A referral event would be an auxiliary service.

GOVERNMENT SERVICE

The quest for knowledge of themselves and their environment has been a paramount concern to scholars since the time of Thales of Miletus (585 BC) to whom the first records of philosophical thinking are credited. [Law 2007] However, the first person to use the term "philosophize," referring to knowledge for its own sake, appears to have been used by Herodotus [Fullerton 2013] in about 484 BC. In many instances, mystical thinking and scientific thought, for example Pythagoras (570 BC), would seem to be at odds, but appears to be indicative of a scholarly stage of evolution. Initially, academic concerns involved questions such as "Where did the universe come from?" and "Why is there anything at all?" Plato (427-347 BC) is recognized by scholars as the first person to take a good look at politics and government, and many of his views are recorded in the writings of Aristotle (384-322 BC) who has arguably the most definitive view on the subject. [Aristotle 330] Modern day concerns include topics such as who is suited to rule and who is naturally not suited to rule, how should government be organized, how should the work of a government be partitioned among executive, deliberative, and judicial branches, what forms should the voice of the people and of the government take, what are our social needs for security and stability, are freedom and privacy the same as they used to be, and what is the nature of rights in an advanced multi-cultural world?

Principles of Government

Even though mankind exhibits a human form, it is defined by a rational nature and a genetic makeup. Man achieves his most advanced development through a public community of government plus people with shared beliefs concerning what is good. That is, they like the same things, have similar beliefs, and possess common interests. Three requisite principles are consent, political participation, and the rights of the individual. Accordingly, there are three ideals necessary to synthesize an appropriate government: the rule of law, the voice of the people, and the social need for security and stability.

Organization

What form authority should take leads to how government should be organized, and who is fit to rule is dependent upon the degree to which reason determines the leader's behavior. Theoretically, a system of departments, or offices, determines a collective typically engaged with providing service to its constituents. Methods of appointment and the tenure of office are historically of concern, but from a service perspective, the structure of the collective trumps the individuals and their method of management. The degree of interaction between departments is of prime importance.

Freedom and The Rule of Law

It is clear that the rule of law is necessary for a just and stable society, but the exact form that this form of justice should take is and has been a matter of concern. The fact that laws should be fair and non-oppressive and how the leaders in government are chosen are generally known and supported by even the casual observer of modern society. However, our lives are intertwined with others, some of whom are known intimately, others casually, and still others that we will never know. Our behavior towards those individuals should be considered from at least two viewpoints: our rights and our responsibilities.

Freedom is the right of the citizen to act and speak as they choose without interference from the state. [Law op cit., p. 162] Typically, freedom, as such, involves freedom of movement, freedom of choice, freedom of religion, freedom of speech, and so forth. The boundary to freedom is raised when it is used to harm others. Two aspects of freedom are the harm principle and the concept of a neutral state. In simple terms, the freedom to do something is more important than what they do. Thus, people can make different choices and, in so doing, some will win and some will lose, leading to inequality.

Individual freedom of this sort is generally known as *liberalism*. In our society, the government is a sort of neutral umpire between persons with different goals and different choices.

As one might expect, liberalism has two forms: libertarianism and social democracy. Libertarians believe in basic services from government and no more. Social democracy views the government as a means of providing an equal and just society and uses rights as a means of providing the requisite equality. Social democracy believes in ensuring equality of opportunity and not outcome. Obviously, social democracy is more expensive than libertarianism, and the extra money must come from taxes.

It follows that a service of the government with social democracy is to provide equal freedom for all and it must intervene and make education, health-care, and welfare available to all. The liberal view is commonly based on the notion of rights as a non-negotiable claim to a service, usually provided by a government.

Negative and Positive Rights

Rights are an important part of government and professional services and can be viewed in different ways. With regard to service, we are going to focus on positive, negative, legal, moral, claim and liberty rights. A *negative right* is a right that is not to be denied by the action of another person or group, and a *positive right* is a right that takes advantage of the actions of another person or group. Thus, a right is a privilege owned by an individual. In the domain of services, there are two sides to the story: providers and clients. Any rights associated with service providers can be classed as legal rights. Rights associated with service clients are generally classed as claim or liberty rights.

Legal rights are those rights determined by existing legal statutes. Moral rights are rights that usually exist prior to their legal counterpart. Moral rights are moral claims that could eventually be assimilated into the legal system. Legal rights derive from certification, qualification, and registration. Moral rights derive from a derivative of claim and liberty rights. It seems as though one person's right is another entities responsibilities. A right is commonly regarded as a freedom, which limits the benefit of the community. Therefore, it is sometimes prudent to limit the extent of personal freedom for the common good.

One means of considering rights is that they provide a framework for determining the basic economic, political, and social conditions required for individuals to lead a good life. [Fagan 2005] Through a convention of some sort, a service provider has a legal right to provide a service within a specific domain, and a service client has a claim right against the provider to supply the object of that right. Thus, a claim right is an expectation that a client has concerning a duty a provider is expected to provide. A liberty right refers to a duty that no one else is required to provide. [Fagan op cit.]

Government Intentionality

As a structured entity with diverse responsibilities, a government – regardless of its size and mission – is a collective, as defined previously. The notion that a collective entity, such as a government, could have a set of collective beliefs and subsequent intents might seem controversial to persons who believe that individuals alone can have beliefs and intents, requiring a mind or a brain. [Tollefsen 2004] During periods of intense stress, such as a war, it is customary to establish a consensual view through planning and propaganda. Of course, this is to be expected, in unusual conditions, but as a general rule, there are those who seriously doubt that the concept has a definitive role in everyday affairs.

On the other hand, individuals often act in concert with others as a form of group behavior and thereby permit inherent action to be explained and predicted. This form of endeavor – known in Philosophy as "collective intentionality" – attempts to explain how organizations can be held morally or legally responsible for their actions. When an organization, such as that which is inherent in the following quote, "The Defense Department reports that a reduction in troop levels will reduce our security level," we are speaking metaphorically, based perhaps on a desired end state, rather than a collective intent.

There are different approaches for describing a collective intent, and individual action seems to be at the core of such discussions. Two summative accounts have been offered: simple summative account (SSA) and complex summative account (CSA). [Gilbert 1987] With SSA, a collective specification takes the form:

Group G believes that p if and only if all or most of the members believe that p.

Consider the case where the government decides to give a large amount of money to a foreign government, especially when the "giving" government has a budget crisis, and that most of the population is against giving the assistance. The voters do not voice this opinion because of the negative reaction that would be received from their associates. Accordingly, it would appear that the population is in favor of giving the financial support, which is not necessarily the case. Perhaps, there is no equitable means of voicing a negative opinion. With CSA that takes the form:

> A group G believes that p if and only if (1) most of the members of G believe that p, and (2) it is common knowledge in G of (1).

Thus, CSA is a stronger approach, even though Gilbert thinks that both SSA and CSA are generally insufficient [Gilbert op cit.] and that a plural subject – that is, a collection of individuals that believe as a body – is required wherein each person involved has a conceptual grasp of the subject matter. So, what does this have to do with service? It would seem that the actions of government in a service environment operate with a requisite level of transparency. A related topic related to government intentionality is consequentialism, in the which the result of actions of a plural subject in covered. [Haines 2006]

Existentialism and Service

Metaphysics is commonly regarded as a subject that explores the nature of reality. An associated subject is *existentialism* that concerns the actual experience of being human. Much of related study is based on the work of Heidegger, who proposed the concept of "being there." [Law op cit., p. 328] One of the difficulties with the subject of service is that – at least as far as the literature is concerned – it emphasizes a "bird's eye" view of the topic. As a noted orthopedic surgeon is quoted about service science, "I don't do that kind of thing." A suitable response was, "If not, then what?"

One of the major problems in government, education, and business is that persons involved do not recognize that they are in the service business, and there are no norms that cover what good service is.

SUMMARY

It is generally recognized that *service* is a provider/client collaboration that creates and captures value for both participants. Both entities contribute in the interchange and both benefit, even though the sense of participation is diverse and varies between different forms of service execution. An example is the relationship between a doctor and patient that relies on the participation of both persons, since both entities are required in order for the service to be instantiated. Moreover, a doctor's service varies between patients and yields different results, depending on the situation. This characteristic is typical of most service. The entity supplying the service is known as the *service provider* and the entity receiving the service is known as the *service client*. The domain of service providers includes individuals, teams, products, electronic systems, groups, and ad hoc units organized to execute a particular service delivery scenario. Similarly, service clients include persons, groups, social organizations, governments, and commercial entities. In some cases, the object receiving the service is the responsibility of the client, as in cleaning and repair services. In this instance, the entity receiving the service is known as the *service object*.

Most governmental activity involves service, yet very little is known about the subject. This paper offers a brief look at government services, as well as a look at some interesting problems. The relationship between service and government is explored as a basis for the study of service and government.

REFERENCES

[1] Aristotle. (Aristotéles Stageirta, born in Stagira, Macedonia – now Greece in 384 BCE), *Politics*, New York: Barnes & Noble, 2005. (Originally published in 330 BCE, Translated by Benjamin Jowett, Introduction by Joseph Carrig)

[2] Boghossian, P., *Fear of Knowledge: Against Relativism and Constructivism*, Oxford: Oxford University Press, 2006.

[3] Fagan, A., Human Rights, *Internet Encyclopedia of Philosophy*, http://www.iep.utm.edu, 2005.

[4] Fullerton, G., *An Introduction to Philosophy*, London: Pearl Necklace Books, 2013.

[5] Gilbert, M., Modelling Collective Belief, *Synthese*, Vol,73, 1987, (Secondary reference)

[6] Haines, W., Consequentialism, *Internet Encyclopedia of Philosophy*, www.iep.utm.edu, 2006.

[7] Law, S., *Philosophy*, London: Dorling Kindersley, 2007.

[8] Katzan, H., Service Collectivism, Collaboration, and Duality Theory, *IABR Business Conference*, Orlando, FL, 2010.

[9] Katzan, H., *Service Science: Concepts, Technology, Management*, New York: iUniverse, Inc., 2008.

[10] Katzan, H., The K-Factor in Service Analysis, *Proceedings of the Southeast Decision Science Institute Conference*, Charleston, SC, 2009.

[11] Katzan, H., The Role of Government from a Service Perspective, *Proceedings of the Southeast Informs Conference*, Myrtle Beach, SC, 2009.

[12] Maglio, P., An Interdisciplinary Approach to Service Innovation, *IBM Almaden Research Center*, http://almaden.ibm.com/ssme, 2007.

[13] Mannion, J., *Essentials of Philosophy*, New York: Fall River Press, 2002.

[14] Norman, D., *Living with Complexity*, Cambridge, MA: The MIT Press, 2011.

[15] Paine, T. *Common Sense*, New York: Fall River Press, 2013. (Originally published in 1776, Introduction by Gregory Tietjen, 1995)

[16] Smith, A., *The Wealth of Nations*, New York: Barnes and Noble, Inc., 2004, (Originally published as "An Inquiry into the Nature and Causes of the Wealth of Nations" in London England, 1776.)

[17] Tollefsen, D., Collective Intentionality, *Internet Encyclopedia of Philosophy*, http://www.iep.utm.edu, 2004.

***** End 0f Essay 13 *****

About the Author

Professor Harry Katzan, Jr. has written books and papers on computer science and service science and teaches in the graduate program at a major university. He has written *Introduction to Service: What It Is and What It Should Be* and *Service Concepts for Management: A Practical Approach,* both published by iUniverse.

End of Collection of Essays

www.ingramcontent.com/pod-product-compliance
Lightning Source LLC
Chambersburg PA
CBHW020744180526
45163CB00001B/336